THE GREAT WAR:

Remastered WW1 Standard History Collection

Volume 4

This volume collects parts 10-12 of

The Great War: The Standard History of the All-Europe Conflict

October 24, 1914 - November 7, 1914

THE GREAT WAR:

Remastered WW1 Standard History Collection

Volume 4

Collected and designed by Mark Bussler

www.ClassicGameRoom.com

Collect the Entire Series!

The Great War:

Remastered WW1 Standard History Collection

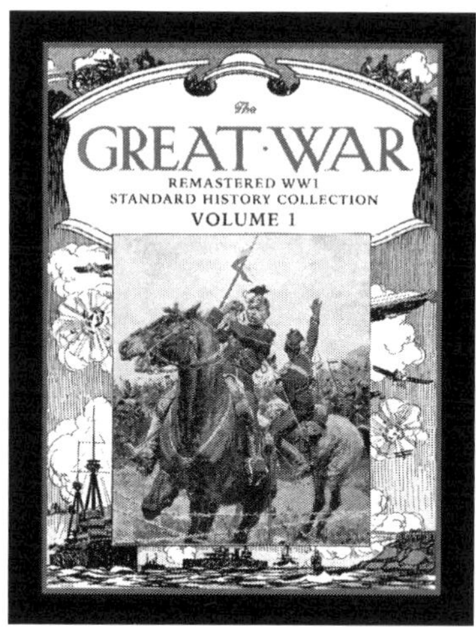

Volume 1: Parts 1-3
August 17, 1914 - August 31, 1914

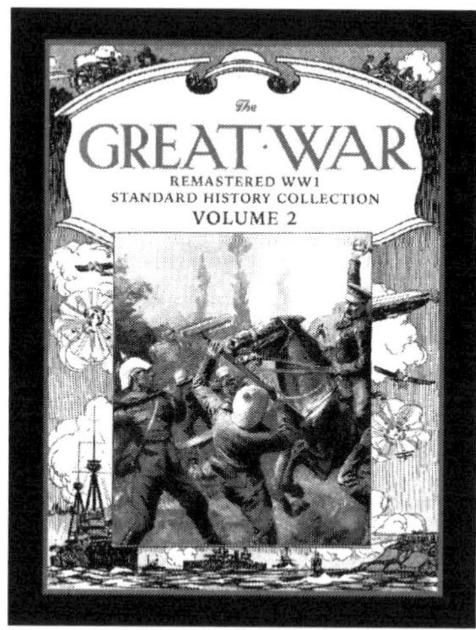

Volume 2: Parts 4-6
September 7, 1914 - September 21, 1914

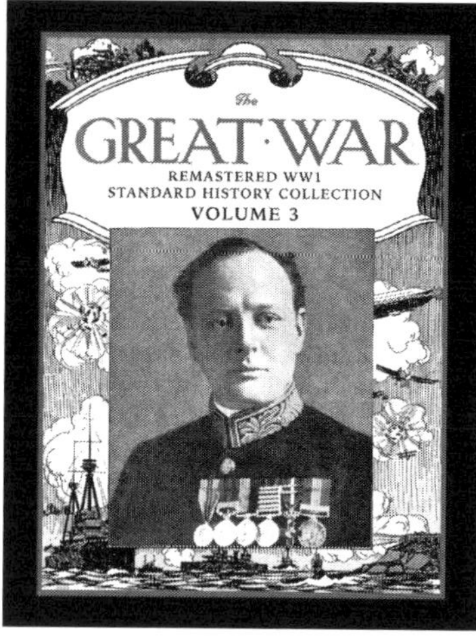

Volume 3: Parts 7-9
September 28, 1914 - October 17, 1914

Volume 4: Parts 10-12
October 24, 1914 - November 7, 1914

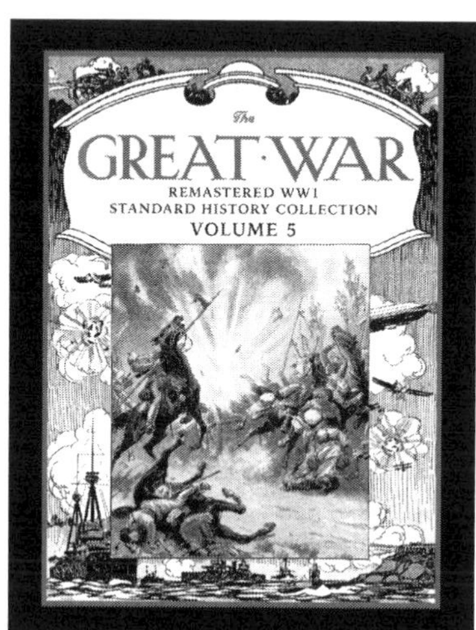

Volume 5: Parts 13-15
November 11, 1914 - November 28, 1914

Volume 6: Parts 16-18
December 5, 1914 - December 19, 1914

...and more!

Week ending October 24th, 1914]

[Registered for Canadian Magazine Post.

Part 10. Reprints of all back parts now on sale. 6d. Net.

The GREAT · WAR

THE STANDARD HISTORY OF THE ALL-EUROPE CONFLICT

Edited by H·W·Wilson, author of

"With the Flag to Pretoria," "Japan's Fight for Freedom," etc.

Albert I., King of the Belgians.

(Photo: W. and D. Downey.)

Make your "Great War" permanent

To make "The Great War" into complete volumes that will be an enduring record of the stupendous conflict to keep and treasure in future years

You - must - have - ALL - the - parts

The demand for the parts preceding this one has been so great that all were sold out, but they have all been reprinted, so that

all - back - parts - are - now - on - sale

The evidence that "The Great War" is regarded as the supreme work of its kind accumulates every day. From British Colonies orders for all past and future parts flow in, and the publishers have been approached with requests to sell translation rights in five foreign countries.

Keep your parts

so that, when the time comes, you can have them bound into handsome, permanent volumes that will adorn your home and constitute a great history classic. Make good any gaps in your collection,

and do it now

before they are out of print

"AMPHION" SURVIVORS, RESCUED FROM THE SEA, REACHING ENGLAND AND SAFETY.

On August 6th, 1914, two days after war opened, the British light cruiser Amphion, after sinking a German mine-layer, fell a victim to floating mines which the mine-layer had strewn in the path of neutral commerce. Of the crew 148 were killed by the explosion or by drowning, and 143 were saved by the Amphion's attending fleet of destroyers. The survivors were landed on the Harwich coast in the plight seen in the picture—hatless, shoeless, and clad only in shirts and trousers. Captain Fox, who commanded the Amphion, was given command of the new flotilla leader Faulknor, one of the two vessels under construction for the Chilian Navy, and taken over by the British Government.

"Three minutes after the captain left his ship another explosion occurred which enveloped and blew up the whole fore part of the vessel. The effects showed that she must have struck a second mine, which exploded the fore magazine. The Amphion was actually sunk in the same way as the battleship Petropavlovsk in the Russo-Japanese War. She struck a cable upon which mines were strung, and the momentum of the ship, though considerably checked by the explosion of the first mine and the stoppage of the engines, was sufficient to carry her against the second mine. Débris falling from a great height struck the rescue boats and destroyers, and one of the Amphion's shells burst on the deck of one of the latter, killing two of the men and a German prisoner rescued from the cruiser.

"The after part now began to settle quickly, till its foremost part was on the bottom, and the whole after part tilted up at an angle of forty-five degrees. In another quarter of an hour this, too, had disappeared. Captain Fox speaks in high terms of the behaviour of officers and men throughout. Every order was promptly obeyed without confusion or perturbation."

A severe test of British seamen

In this brief official statement describing the first British loss of the war—a loss, too, brought about in the most dispiriting and nerve-wrecking of all possible circumstances—the British nation learned again what it already knew in its heart, that the courage, the coolness, and the discipline of the British seaman had not deteriorated from the glorious standard of the past. These men of the Amphion were inspired by none of the enthusiasm and the excitement of battle. Their ship was shattered under them by an unseen enemy—an enemy they could not fight, against which they had no protection.

Yet, after the first shock of the explosion which wrecked the fore part of the ship, everything was carried out as if at manœuvres. The force of the explosion tore the funnels from their bases, and the guns and mountings from their emplacements, and threw them high into the air. The majority of those who lost their lives were mercifully killed outright by the first explosion, and as this occurred right in the bows of the ship, where the men's berths were, the petty officers and men inevitably suffered severely. One hundred and forty-eight of the latter were killed or drowned, together with about twenty German prisoners rescued from the Königin Luise.

The only officer to lose his life was Staff-Paymaster Joseph T. Gedge. A large number of men were injured more or less severely, the majority suffering from burns and scalds caused by the shattering of the boilers and the ignition of the oil fuel which the ship carried in her double bottoms.

FF

General view of the great shipbuilding yards of Blohm and Voss, in Hamburg, which give employment to about 10,000 men.

The turbine machine shop at the engineering yard of Blohm and Voss, Hamburg, who built the Goeben and the Moltke, the world's swiftest battle-cruisers, at the outbreak of hostilities. The famous Vulcan yards are also in Hamburg.

Glimpse of the Imperial Works in Kiel, with the Prinz Heinrich under construction. The upper inset picture shows one of the 150-ton floating cranes used in the Imperial shipyards at Kiel, and the lower inset picture a turbine for a German destroyer, made in the same works.

GERMANY'S WAR PREPARATIONS AT HAMBURG AND KIEL.

How Germany Sowed the High Seas with Mines

The behaviour of the destroyers was not the least heroic part of this unfortunate occurrence. The fact that the Amphion had struck a mine in the area previously passed over by the Königin Luise was proof enough that the whole flotilla was in the midst, or at any rate on the edge, of an invisible mine-field. Yet they all closed in round the doomed ship, lying as close in as they dared, and lowering their boats to pick up the survivors, while all the time the powder and shells in the Amphion's magazine were exploding and turning the wrecked ship into a veritable volcano. It was indeed marvellous that only three men—one of them a German prisoner—should have been killed by the shower of missiles that were thrown over a wide area round the sinking ship.

The great risk to the rescuing ships

The loss of the Amphion—the first warship to be sunk in the war—came not unnaturally as a shock to the people of this country. The material loss, however, was slight, the ship being one of but little fighting power; and it was instantly realised that, bound as we were to prove ultimately successful at sea, the desired end—the annihilation of the enemy's fleet—could not be attained without some sacrifice on our part. There was further consolation in the fact that the Amphion was not sunk in action, but by means of mines sown indiscriminately and illegally on the high seas.

THE BRITISH DESTROYER LARK CONVOYING A PASSENGER STEAMER ACROSS THE CHANNEL.
The destroyer Lark, along with her sister destroyers Lance, Laurel, and Linnet, all acting under Captain Fox on the ill-fated Amphion, chased and sunk the German mine-layer Königin Luise on August 6th, 1914, and helped to save the survivors of the Amphion's crew when the German floating mines had done their deadly work.

As the First Lord of the Admiralty declared in the House of Commons two days after the disaster: "The indiscriminate use of mines, not in connection with military harbours or strategic positions—the indiscriminate scattering of contact mines about the seas, which may destroy not merely enemy vessels or warships, but peaceful merchantmen passing under neutral flags, and possibly carrying supplies to neutral countries—this use of mines is new in warfare, and it deserves to be considered attentively, not only by us who are, of course, engaged in the war, and who may naturally be prone to hasty judgment in such matters, but also by the nations of the civilised world. The Admiralty are not at all alarmed or disconcerted by such incidents. We have expected a certain number, and we continue to expect a certain number of such incidents, and our arrangements provide for reducing such occurrences to the minimum possible."

Indiscriminate use of sea mines

The later experience of the war was to show that, in spite of the great and unceasing efforts made by our Navy to clear the seas of these wildly-scattered mines, Mr. Churchill's expectation that we should lose more ships by their agency was destined to be realised. But the spirit in which the Navy was prepared to face these unseen and shamefully-prepared dangers was nobly exemplified by a brief announcement which the Admiralty issued on the very day following the destruction of the Amphion. It was to the effect that Captain Fox would take command of the new flotilla leader Faulknor, on the completion of that ship, and resume the command of the Third Destroyer Flotilla. The Faulknor was one of two vessels (the other being the Broke) which had been completing in this country for the Chilian Navy, and which the British Admiralty had taken over on the outbreak of war.

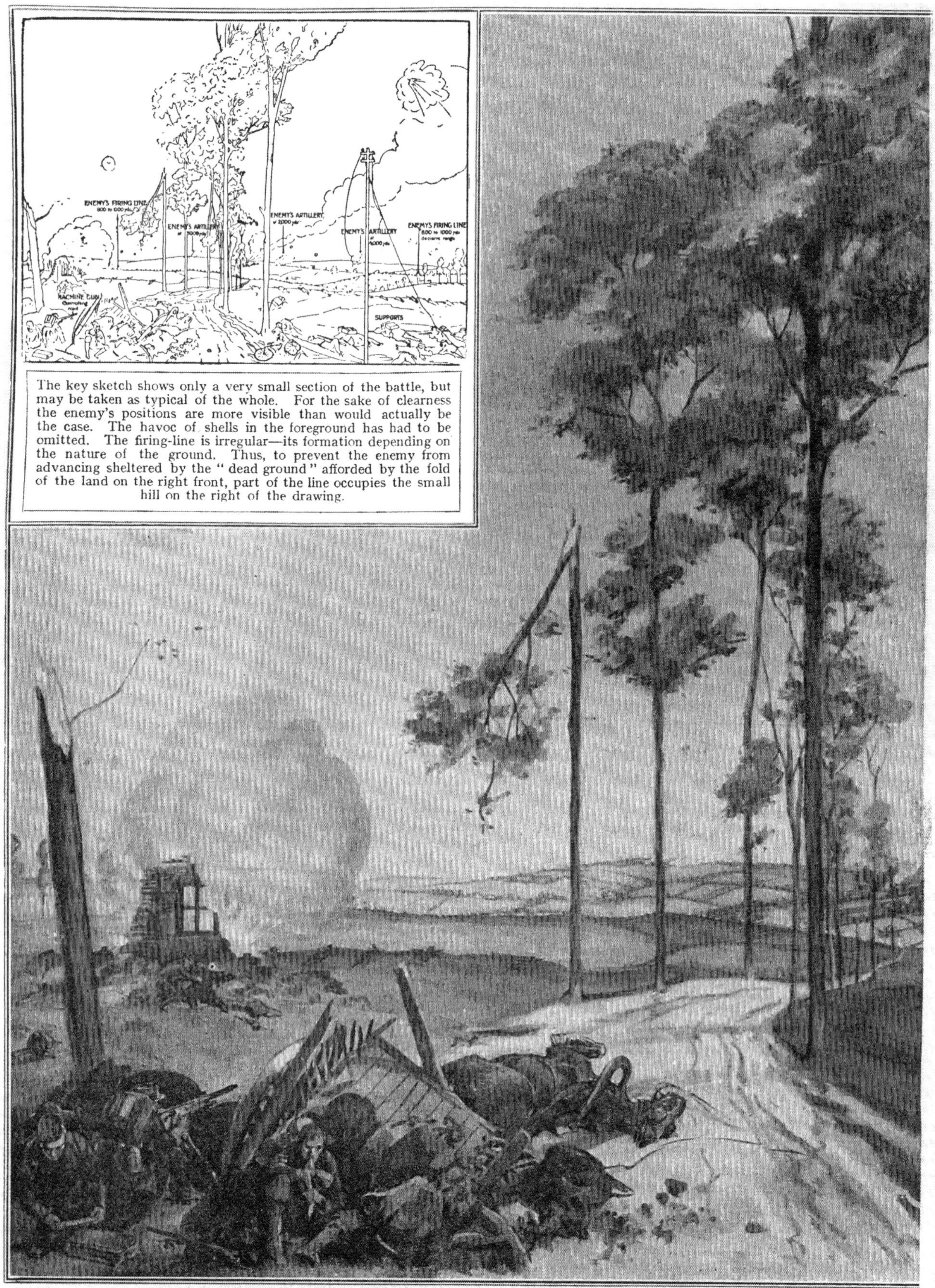

The key sketch shows only a very small section of the battle, but may be taken as typical of the whole. For the sake of clearness the enemy's positions are more visible than would actually be the case. The havoc of shells in the foreground has had to be omitted. The firing-line is irregular—its formation depending on the nature of the ground. Thus, to prevent the enemy from advancing sheltered by the "dead ground" afforded by the fold of the land on the right front, part of the line occupies the small hill on the right of the drawing.

The far-flung battle-line of the world's greatest armed struggle showed war upon a more stupendous scale than ever before. The great "Battle of the Rivers" in Northern France engaged in deadly conflict twenty times the number of combatants that decided the fate of Europe at Waterloo. The modern battle is warfare reduced to a specialised science, which has reached as high a stage of perfection as—or higher than—any of the sciences of peace. The great engines of death, the range of modern artillery and the destructive power of high explosives have robbed war of its picturesque side. The dash of cavalry and the spear-to-breast charges

—ARE DETERMINED BY WEEKS-LONG ARTILLERY DUELS.

THE science of battle has been well explained in the following words:

"The first object of a commander who seeks to gain the initiative in battle is to develop superiority of fire as a preparation for the delivery of a decisive blow. . . . During the process of establishing a superiority of fire, successive fire positions will be occupied by the firing-line. As a rule natural cover will be chosen, but if none exist, and the intensity of the hostile fire precludes any immediate advance, it may be expedient for the firing-line to entrench itself."

The men lie close to the ground, each one seeking what slender cover the folds of the ground afford, and improving his position if possible by such entrenchment as time allows him. Behind, near the spectator, lie the supports, saving their fire till an advance or the deadly effect of the enemy's aim need their presence in the line. Overhead the air is full of the exchange of projectiles from the guns—shrapnel flinging its cone of death on to the combatants. To the rear are reserves at intervals and more reserves; there are also the nerve centres —officers who transmit by messenger or field telephone to the brain (miles behind) the progress of the fight in that small section of the line which is all that they themselves know of the battle.

The road lies empty, a road of death, especially to a man in a dark uniform—it may, perhaps, tempt the enemy's cavalry; but there is a machine-gun hidden by a broken cart, so such an eventuality as that is well provided for. Any ranging mark, such as a building, is carefully avoided if the enemy's guns are about, for if it has not been previously destroyed by the troops in its vicinity the hostile shells will speedily put the matter right.

of infantry are still incidents in a great battle, but subordinate incidents. The main part of a battle consists of a long succession of artillery and rifle duels, where it is the objective of each side to conceal its positions, to protect its combatants, to find the range of the opposing lines, and to deal out death by an accurate and overwhelming fire of heavy guns, machine-guns, and rifles, so that the enemy is compelled to evacuate his position, or is so weakened that he is no longer able to resist effectively the charge of cavalry or the cold steel of an infantry attack.

The significance of this picture is explained by the diagram above.

THE NORTH GERMAN LLOYD PRINZ FRIEDRICH WILHELM.

CHAPTER XV.

HOW GERMANY ATTACKED OUR COMMERCE.

The Growth of Germany's Mercantile Marine—Fostered by Subsidy—Economic Value of the British Navy—Importance of Food Imports to Great Britain—Disposition of British Fleet at Outbreak of War—The Navies of our Dominions—German Naval Disposition and Coaling Stations—Policy of Arming Merchant Vessels—Britain's Grip Upon Germany's Ocean Communications—How Wireless Telegraphy Helped in Naval War—Fear for Food Famine in First Days of War—Treatment of Hostile Ships—Disturbance in Insurance Market—British Government Relieves the Situation—Operations of the German Dresden against Allied Shipping—Adventures and Fate of the Kaiser Wilhelm der Grosse and the Bethania—The Value of Speed in Naval Raids—The Allies' Command of the Sea.

WHEN the German Empire was founded the total tonnage of the merchant ships flying the black, white, and red flag of the German mercantile marine was 982,355, and in eighteen years—that is, by the time that Wilhelm II. became Emperor—it had increased by no more than 300,000 tons. But the new ruler soon let it be known that he regarded the development of the mercantile marine as one of his most cherished ambitions. At the same time, he never failed to emphasise the fact that a great merchant navy could have no permanent existence without a powerful war fleet to protect it and to assist in its expansion.

The development of German merchant shipping was considerably aided by the payment of subsidies, which enabled the companies in receipt of them to carry goods at low rates and so take trade from their competitors. The loss, if any, was made up by the Imperial Government. At the same time, great encouragement was given by various artificial means to the expansion of the shipbuilding industry. The effect of these measures is plainly visible in the great strides which have been made. In 1870 the German mercantile marine stood fifth in order of tonnage among the merchant navies of the world, but by the beginning of the present century it was second, surpassed only by the British Empire, and it has since continued to improve its position. In 1870 there were approximately seven and a half tons of merchant shipping under the British flag for every one under the German, but by 1912 the proportion was only a little over four tons to one in our favour, the actual figures being: British Empire, 13,846,365 tons; Germany, 3,153,724 tons.

THE GERMAN 3,600-TON CRUISER DRESDEN,
which is the sister ship of the Emden, and which sunk the British merchantmen Hyades and City of Winchester in South American waters soon after war began.

Nevertheless, the British mercantile marine remained by far the greatest and the most important, but with every ton added to it the maritime risks of the Empire were increased. The task of our ships was to carry our trade between these islands and countries oversea, and to bring to the teeming millions of our country those supplies of food and raw material which we are unable to produce for ourselves. Every additional ship was a hostage to fortune—a further indication of the ever-increasing dependence of Great Britain upon

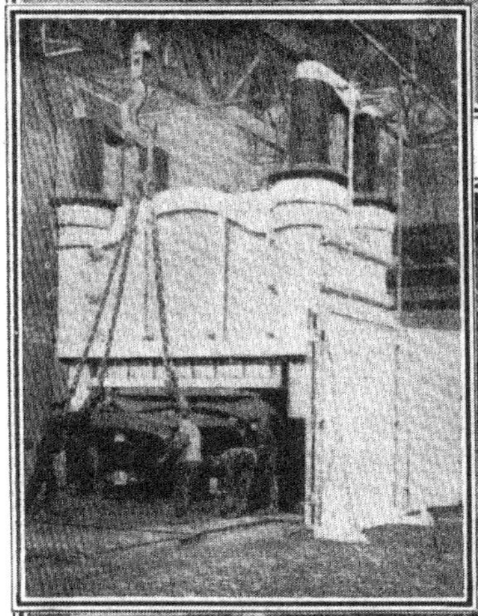

General view of Krupp's Germania shipbuilding works at Kiel. The vicious Krupp interests dominated the Kaiser and German Imperial policy, being indeed the chief primary cause of the war.

General view of the fitting and finishing shop in a large German armament manufactory. The biggest German naval gun is 15 in. diameter and throws a projectile of 1,675 lb. weight. The inset picture shows an armour plate being bent under a 10,000-ton hydraulic press.

An iron foundry in the Germania shipbuilding works of the great Krupp firm at Kiel. The other private yard at Kiel is owned by the firm of Howaldt, but the Imperial yard employs as many men—about ten thousand—as the two private yards combined.

THE MAKING OF GERMANY'S SHIPS AND GUNS AT KIEL.

WHERE SOME OF GERMANY'S FINEST BATTLESHIPS WERE BUILT.
The entrance to the Imperial shipbuilding yards at Kiel, which before the war employed about 10,000 men. The hanging bridge is a wonderful piece of engineering, the towers being 200 feet high and 400 feet apart, while the "ferry" is suspended by steel cables and operated by electricity. The waterway is always open for the largest ships to pass, and the ferry traffic is possible at all times except during the actual minutes that a ship is entering. Kiel, a fortified town of about 150,000, is one of the best havens in Europe, and is Germany's chief war port. It is the headquarters of the German Navy, with a naval academy and a university.

the command of the sea. Owing to the success with which the British Navy kept the trade routes open during the Great War it is doubtful whether even now we realise the complete dependence of our country upon its maritime trade. This could only be adequately brought home to us by the defeat of the Navy.

The bulk of the workmen in this country are dependent for their weekly wage upon the importation of raw material and the export of the manufactured article, and the failure of the Navy to keep open the trade routes would mean a wholesale closing down of factories and workshops, and particularly of those great firms in the North which rely upon the regular delivery of the raw materials of the cotton, wool, and other textile industries imported to the annual value of £150,000,000.

The question of food is not less important than the question of work and wages Year by year we are becoming less and less able to feed ourselves. Thousands of acres of land have passed out of cultivation and thousands of workers have left the land for the manufacturing centres, and by so doing have increased the dependence of the country upon the command of the sea.

THE BIRTHPLACE OF BRITAIN'S GUNS.
The main gate of Woolwich Arsenal, where, in times of great pressure, 20,000 men work day and night manufacturing artillery

The latest available figures show that we import food to the annual value of £280,000,000 a year. This means that every day of the year food to the value of £780,000 is landed in our ports. It means that if our Navy were unable to protect the ocean highways along which hundreds of British merchantmen are daily ploughing their way we should starve. How long we could exist if these supplies were cut off has been variously estimated. It might be as long as three months if we had our harvest in hand. It might be as short as three weeks if the catastrophe overtook us at a less favourable moment. In any case, the stoppage of our sea-borne trade would inevitably mean disaster—universal unemployment followed by universal starvation.

Nations which have contemplated war with Great Britain have reckoned not a little upon the damage which they would be able to inflict upon us by interfering with our merchant shipping, and they did so with fairly good reason. They argued from the experience of the wars of the French Revolution, when the price of wheat rose to treble the peace figure. During the twenty years from 1793 to 1812 we lost no fewer than 10,871 merchant ships, an average of 543 a year. As our merchant shipping is far greater now than it was then, and as we are dependent to an infinitely greater extent upon the security of our merchant shipping, both for food and for trade, it was freely assumed, both by British thinkers and by our enemies, that the attack of British commerce offered the surest means of bringing this country to its knees. There is not the slightest doubt that any serious interference with our merchant shipping would have been followed by disaster at home.

THE FAMOUS "GOLD SHIP"—THE KRONPRINZESSIN CECILIE.
On July 28th, 1914, this great 19,500-ton North German Lloyd liner left New York for Germany carrying gold to the value of £2,000,000 for the Bank of England, and when nearing Europe she received a wireless message from Germany advising her to avoid the English Channel and try to reach her home port via the North of Scotland, but she was afraid of capture and steamed back to America, where she entered Bar Harbour, Maine, on the morning of August 5th, and had to remain inactive during the war. Attempts to sell her along with other German ships to American owners have failed on account of the opposition of the anti-German allies.

The safeguarding of British trade

It was not alone upon the actual work of their cruisers at sea that our prospective enemies depended. They also assumed that on the mere approach of war British shipowners would be appalled at the prospect of their vessels being sunk or captured by the warships of the enemy, and would lay their vessels up in harbour rather than expose them to this risk. Infinite reliance was placed upon the assumed "nervousness" of British shipping. It was the very general belief in this country that even in the most favourable circumstances the opening weeks of a war with a strong naval Power would see the cost of food advance to almost prohibitive prices, which might, or might not, be reduced as time went on by the increasing success of the British Navy in running down the enemy's commerce destroyers. That this protective work might be begun with the least possible delay, squadrons of British cruisers were maintained throughout the nineteenth century in various parts of the world, so as to be immediately available in the event of war to safeguard British trade passing through the areas which it was their duty to patrol.

THE TREMENDOUS FORCE OF A SEA-MINE EXPLOSION.
A graphic representation of the effect caused by exploding a submarine mine. The fate of a great ship that has the ill-fortune to strike one of these mines can be understood from the gigantic upheaval caused by the explosion as seen above. At first, our Government refrained from sowing the sea with mines, and announced on August 23rd, 1914, that no mines had up to that time been laid, but on October 3rd it was officially stated that mines had been laid in a specified area in the southern part of the North Sea, chiefly to protect the approaches to the Thames.

In the ten years immediately preceding the outbreak of war these squadrons had, unfortunately, been grievously reduced. The rapid increase in the strength of the German Navy in the North Sea led the British Admiralty to weaken greatly the force of the British Navy in distant seas, in order that the ships and men thus released might be used to strengthen our fleet in home waters.

On the eve of the outbreak of war our principal naval forces on foreign stations outside Europe were composed as follows:

In the East Indies, one old battleship and two light cruisers.

In the Far East, one old battleship, two armoured cruisers, two light cruisers and eight destroyers.

At the Cape of Good Hope, three light cruisers, all slow and obsolete.

On the Pacific Coast of America, two ancient sloops.

On the South-East Coast of America, one light cruiser.

On the West Coast of Africa, one gunboat.

On the Atlantic Coast of North America, four armoured cruisers and one light cruiser.

Besides these ships, the naval forces of Australia, New Zealand, and Canada were placed at the disposal of the Admiralty immediately on the outbreak of war. Of these the Australian Fleet was by far the most important. It included the battle-cruiser Australia, the flagship, and two other modern sea-going vessels in the light cruisers Sydney and Melbourne, these three ships being all capable of steaming twenty-five knots. There were two older cruisers, a few coast defence craft, three destroyers, and two submarines. Canada had never attempted to carry out a definite naval policy, and the only warships she was able to hand over to the Imperial Government were two old ships which she had bought a few years before with the object of training her own personnel and establishing a Canadian Navy. As soon as war was declared she purchased a couple of submarines that were building at San Francisco for the Chilian Navy, and so added two useful units to the defence of the Pacific Coast.

New Zealand was only able to hand over three ancient cruisers to the Admiralty, but we must not forget that this patriotic Dominion had already presented the Empire with a ship equal in power to the Australia. This vessel, the New Zealand, was to have been stationed as flagship in the Far East, but, at the request of the Admiralty, New Zealand permitted her to be kept in European waters, where she figures in the battle order of the Grand Fleet.

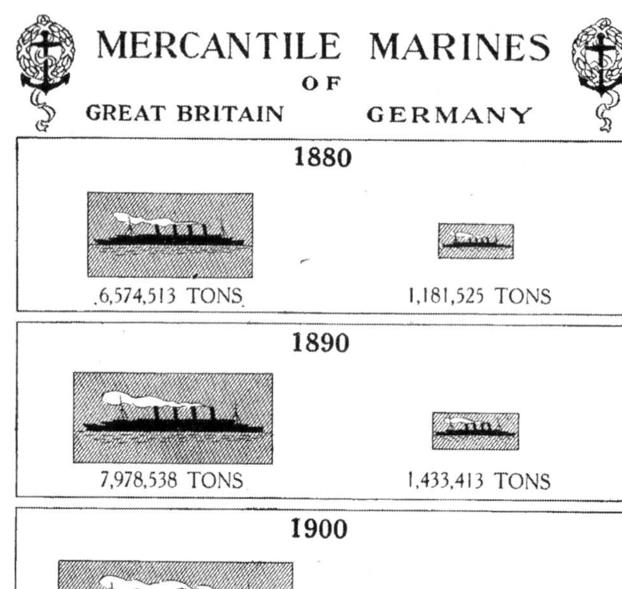

The parallelograms in this chart are drawn to scale, and they illustrate the growth and comparative importance of the British and German mercantile fleets since the year 1880. The British tonnage does not include colonial shipping, which would add about two million tons to the 1912 figures if included. They help to expose the fallacy of the German contention that Germany's merchant fleets required a protecting navy equal in number and power to the British Navy.

Altogether there were about twenty British ships of the cruising classes on foreign stations immediately before the outbreak of war, and only six of these were capable of high speed. There were many eminent naval authorities who looked back to the last great naval wars, when we had been compelled to keep nearly five hundred cruising ships in commission, and predicted that the Admiralty was following a policy which would lead to disaster, and that hostile cruisers would be able to inflict immense loss on our commerce at the outset.

So far as could be discovered from the disposition of her warships, Germany did not place any great reliance upon commerce destroying as a means of bringing about the downfall of this country. Indeed, General von Bernhardi, in his much-discussed book, "Germany and the Next War," said that although the war against British commerce must be boldly and energetically prosecuted, and should start unexpectedly, he nevertheless saw that Germany would have an almost impossible task before her, and that "no very valuable results can be expected from a war against England's trade."

LUDERITZ BAY, COALING STATION OF GERMAN SOUTH-WEST AFRICA, CONTAINS COPPER MINES AND DIAMOND FIELDS.

GERMAN COLONIAL SOLDIER ASTRIDE A ZEBRA AT DAR-ES-SALAAM, COALING-STATION OF GERMAN EAST AFRICA.

APIA, THE CAPITAL OF GERMAN SAMOA.

A STREET IN LOME, THE PORT OF TOGOLAND.

TSING-TAU, PORT OF KIAO-CHAU, WHICH GERMANY SEIZED FROM CHINA, AND JAPAN BLOCKADED ON AUGUST 24, 1914.

Any nation that aspires to maritime power must possess, at various strategic points, stations where her vessels can obtain the coal or oil which enables them to keep the sea. After the outbreak of war Germany was gradually relieved of her coaling-stations. The first to go was the Port of Lome, in Togoland, containing a valuable wireless-telegraphy station, captured on August 8th, 1914. Togoland completely surrendered on August 26th. Apia, in German Samoa, interesting as the burial-place of R. L. Stevenson, the novelist, was surrendered to a New Zealand force on August 30th. Germany's oldest colonial possession was acquired in 1884. Altogether her dependencies, before the war, totalled 1,027,820 square miles, their white population numbering 24,389, and their native population 12,041,603.

The most powerful squadron which Germany kept on a foreign station in time of peace was that in the Far East, which consisted of two armoured and three light cruisers, and a number of gunboats. In the Indian Ocean was one fast cruiser. There were also a couple of old ships in the South Pacific, and four fast vessels in the Atlantic. The British forces immediately available for the attack on these German ships were greatly superior in numbers, though in fast ships Germany outstripped us. We had an enormous advantage, however, in the continuous line of British ports and coaling stations which extends round the globe, while Germany could boast no more than five bases outside the North Sea. These were Kiao-Chau in the Far East, Samoa in the Pacific, Dar-es-Salaam in East Africa, Lüderitz Bay in South-West Africa, and Lome in Togoland, on the West Coast of Africa.

The value of coaling stations

In her plans for the attack of British commerce Germany had to allow for the ease with which these few coaling stations could be masked or captured by squadrons of British cruisers. We shall see later how she overcame this difficulty.

Besides the regular cruisers of her fighting Navy, Germany had made preparations for fitting out a large number of merchant ships with guns and naval crews, and commissioning them on the outbreak of war for commerce destruction. This it was legitimate for her to do, although the same difficulties of coaling and replenishing stores which faced her regular cruisers would apply also to these armed merchantmen. But she also laid plans in another direction, which can best be described in the words that Mr. Churchill used in the House of Commons in March, 1913. " It was made clear at the Second Hague Conference and at the London Conference," he said, " that certain of the Great Powers had reserved to themselves the right to convert merchant steamers into cruisers, not merely in national harbours, but if necessary on the high seas. There is now good reason to believe that a considerable number of foreign merchant steamers may be rapidly converted into armed ships by the mounting of guns.

BERLIN CELEBRATES SEDAN DAY.

September 2nd is " Sedan Day," the blackest day in the French calendar, and the anniversary of the crowning disaster of the Franco-German War. The German armies tried hard to achieve a greater Sedan on September 2nd, 1914, but no such fortune attended their arms, and they had to content themselves by celebrating the first Von Moltke's great triumph by pulling in procession through the streets of Berlin guns captured from France and Russia during the opening weeks of the greater war.

The arming of merchant ships

" The sea-borne trade of the world follows well-marked routes, upon nearly all of which the tonnage of the British mercantile marine largely predominates. Our food-carrying liners and vessels carrying raw material following these trade routes would in certain contingencies meet foreign vessels armed and equipped in the manner described. If the British ships had no armament they would be at the mercy of any foreign liners carrying one effective gun and a few rounds of ammunition."

Mr. Churchill went on to say that it would be obviously absurd to meet this menace by building cruisers in numbers equal to those of the armed merchantmen, and described a scheme by which a number of British food-

From the painting by John St. Helier Lander.

GENERAL SIR HORACE LOCKWOOD SMITH-DORRIEN G.C.B., D.S.O.

One of our ablest military leaders, Sir Horace Smith-Dorrien more than justified his appointment to high command in the British Expeditionary Force. He enhanced a reputation already high by his masterly conduct of the retreat of his army corps from Mons during the memorable week ending August 29th, 1914. In his historic dispatch of September 7th, Sir John French expressed his high appreciation of General Smith-Dorrien's services to his country in these words: "I cannot close the brief account of this glorious stand of the British troops without putting on record my deep appreciation of the valuable services rendered by General Sir Horace Smith-Dorrien. I say without hesitation that the saving of the left wing of the army under my command on the morning of August 26th could never have been accomplished unless a commander of rare and unusual coolness, intrepidity, and determination had been present to personally conduct the operation."

H 11

THE UNQUENCHABLE CHEERFULNESS OF THE BRITISH SOLDIER THAT

THE cost of war is great, not only in money, but in what to a nation is more than money—her glorious manhood.

When a country enters war with a high purpose and with her conscience clean she can face the loss with fortitude and reckon the result well worth the cost. Mr. Asquith, in his great speech at Edinburgh, on September 18th, 1914, expressed the opinion of the Army, the Navy, the nation, and the Empire when, speaking of those who had fallen in the cause, he said: "We shall not mourn them too much. One crowded hour of glorious life is worth an age without a name."

THE figures in this picture, sketched by our artist, who was a spectator of the scene at Waterloo Station, London, are expressive of the spirit that wins great battles, and "wins through" to victory. A contingent of British infantry was entraining for the field of war, and at the same moment a trainload of British wounded drew up at the opposite platform.

The camaraderie of arms and enthusiasm for the work in hand inspired the men as they greeted each other. The sight of those who carried home the wounds of battle was the touch of nature that aroused all the kinship of a common cause, and cheer after cheer was sent across the thronging platform, to be sent back again in feebler tones, but with as high an enthusiasm.

IT was announced officially on August 30th that reinforcements amounting to double the loss suffered to that date had joined the British Expeditionary Force, and this appeared to be the policy upon which the Army authorities acted in the matter of making good the gaps in the ranks during the early stages of the war before it was possible to augment considerably the strength of the fighting arm. The artist has tried to convey that idea into his work.

The ineradicable British habit of enjoying the sporting side of everything—even of war—invested the discomforts of trench work and the hardships of the camp with an interest that overcame all obstacles and disconcerted the attacking foe.

THE DARING HORSEMANSHIP OF THE DREADED COSSACKS.

As fighters on horseback, the Cossacks have always had a personal ascendency over all other cavalry, and in the Great War of the Nations they maintained that ascendency. This scene shows them standing in stirrups crossed over the saddles and swimming their horses across a river. The Cossacks hold their land by a military service tenure, and are liable to duty for life. Service begins at the age of nineteen and lasts for twenty-four years in three distinct periods. First, there is three years' training in their home settlements, followed by twelve years in regimental headquarters. The second is a "home" furlough period, when the man keeps his horse and equipment ready for service, with a short term of training annually. Then there is a four-year period, when the Cossack is required only to keep his arms and equipment ready for service, with one training term of three weeks. Finally, for five years he is in the Reserves, and is only called upon for war service.

carrying ships using the trade routes most likely to be threatened would be armed, "for purposes of self-defence," with two 4·7 in. guns mounted in the stern. By the time that war came, about forty ships had been armed in this way. Their equipment would not have been the slightest use to them in the event of their being attacked by a regular cruiser, or even by a merchant cruiser commissioned in the ordinary way, but it was believed that it would be sufficient to repel the attack of any vessel commissioned in the manner which the First Lord of the Admiralty had described.

BELGIAN SOLDIERS LYING IN WAIT FOR GERMAN PATROLS BEHIND HASTILY-CONSTRUCTED STREET DEFENCES.

Mr. Churchill was hotly attacked by the friends of Germany in England, who pretended to doubt whether a ship not properly commissioned and not under the control of its Government was, in international law, entitled to fire a gun, even in self-defence. In the early stages of the war the United States Government issued a proclamation to the effect that, as these vessels were virtually warships, they would not be allowed to use American ports. Subsequently, however, the embargo was removed, on condition that the

BELGIAN ARTILLERY IN ACTION at Audogom, ten miles north of Alost.

HAVOC CAUSED BY THE GERMAN SIEGE ARTILLERY ON THE OUTER FORTIFICATIONS OF NAMUR.
After the heroic defence of Liège, and its successful arrest of the German advance for three weeks, it was anticipated that a similar defence would be offered by the Belgian fortress of Namur, but the heavy German siege-guns made havoc of it, and it fell on August 24th, 1914. This photograph was taken in one of the trenches of Namur, and illustrates the awful destruction wrought by the German artillery.

guns were of not more than 6 in. calibre, that they were mounted aft, and that the crew of the ship was not increased in consequence of their being mounted.

The most effective defence of British shipping, and the most deadly attack on that of our enemy, however, was provided by the Grand Fleet at home. A glance at a map will show that the British Isles lie like an enormous breakwater across the seaward communications of Germany. Excepting vessels engaged in the Baltic trade and in local coastwise traffic, every ship desiring to enter a German port has to pass near the shores of the British Isles.

The first measure which the British Navy took when war became inevitable was to move to its war stations. Although no one knew at the time where the fleets had gone, everyone knew what was the task they had set out to perform. They had gone to set a final seal upon the naval communications of Germany by holding in force the English Channel and what is known as the "north-about" route into the North Sea—the route that leads round the coast of Scotland to the German seaboard. The effect of this, when war broke out, was that no German ship, whether war vessel or trader, could enter or leave the North Sea without running the gauntlet of the British Navy. A few vessels may have succeeded in getting through by hugging the coast of Norway, and hiding during the day in the numerous fjords by which those shores are so picturesquely scarred; but for all practical purposes the grip of the British Fleet upon the oceanic communications of Germany was complete. By this disposition of our forces the maritime trade of Germany was brought to a standstill. Such vessels as were actually at sea had to choose between seeking the shelter of a neutral port and being captured by British cruisers. Those already in neutral ports were, wherever possible, warned by wireless to remain there; and those in German ports were unable to get out. By this same disposition our enemies were prevented from making any considerable addition to the forces available for the attack on British trade. One or two vessels, among them the Kaiser Wilhelm der Grosse, were certainly added to the cruiser squadron in the Atlantic, but in all probability these got out of the North Sea before war was declared, and before our own ships had any power to stop them. As for the merchant cruisers and armed merchantmen, upon which Germany was relying to no small extent, there is good reason to believe that many of these carried their guns and mountings permanently on board, and that ammunition was shipped from transports either at sea or, what is more likely, in neutral harbours.

Britain's grip on German sea routes

Wireless telegraphy was one of the new factors in the war against commerce, and was expected to play an important part in both the attack and the defence of commerce. After the first few days of war there was practically no German commerce left at sea for our ships to attack, and their energies were therefore

TYPES OF KRUPP GUNS IN USE BY THE GERMAN ARMY.

The mules are carrying portions of a 12-pounder Krupp mountain gun, one of them carrying the gun itself, and the second the mounting, while a third and a fourth mule, not seen in the picture, carry the shield and the ammunition respectively. The centre picture shows a Krupp 12-pounder anti-aircraft gun in position for firing, and the gun in the lowest photograph is an 11 in. Krupp howitzer with its motor-tractor.

TROPHIES OF WAR CAPTURED BY BOTH SIDES.

At the top is a view of the main street in Cologne, where guns captured from the French are on exhibition; in the centre we have a glimpse of the barracks at Liege, in the hands of the Germans, with guns captured from the Belgians; and the third picture shows the Place Royale, in Nancy, where thirty guns taken from the Germans in Alsace are displayed.

concentrated upon hunting down the vessels which Germany had sent to sea for the destruction of our own merchantmen. With the assistance of wireless, merchantmen so equipped would be able to communicate at once to the nearest British warship the whereabouts of any hostile ship that might be encountered. We found later on that, whenever a German cruiser fell in with a defenceless British merchant ship, her first action was to threaten the ship with instant destruction if any single letter was signalled by its wireless operator. In those vessels which German cruisers stopped and boarded, but did not destroy, the wireless apparatus was invariably rendered useless, so that the whereabouts of the hostile ship could not be communicated.

We were also to find that, although in certain circumstances wireless telegraphy was a considerable assistance to our ships in their work, the Germans were frequently able, by tapping and decoding our messages, to secure information enabling them both to waylay our merchant ships and to elude our cruisers. In order to prevent the leakage of news near home, the whole of the wireless service was taken over by the Government before the outbreak of war, and all privately-owned stations were ordered to be dismantled. Concurrently with the declaration of hostilities, an order was issued prohibiting the employment of wireless by all ships (with, of course, the exception of warships) in home waters. But the Germans were able to obtain much information through neutral wireless stations in the United States, in South America, and in the Dutch East Indies.

Fears for our food supply

In spite of the excellent reasons we had for believing in the ability of the British Navy to keep the trade routes clear and so to maintain an uninterrupted supply of food from oversea, the first few days of war led to something very much like a panic both in shipping circles, where reliance on the power of the Navy should have been highest, and among the general public. Perhaps the real reason for this state of affairs lay not so much in distrust of the Fleet as in ignorance of its strength and organisation.

There was a wild rush for food supplies. Those who gave way to alarm honestly believed that provisions would, in a very short time, be forced up to famine prices. They proceeded to spend as much as they could afford upon the purchase of stocks sufficient to last them for months. Even the big stores were cleared out of their supplies of tinned milk and preserved meats, and in outlying districts flour became almost unprocurable.

The British Isles athwart Germany's path

Ministers appealed to the people to take things calmly, assuring them that there was no cause for alarm; then the panic was allayed, and prices began to settle down again. The alarmists, including several British newspapers, which published horrifying articles before the war as to the risk of famine, were surprised to discover that food ships were arriving at our ports almost as regularly as if war did not exist. Within a week or two the cost of food had sunk almost to its normal level. Those who had rushed in with huge orders for potted meats and comestibles found their larders loaded with all sorts of provisions which in the ordinary course they could not eat, and which had been bought at inflated prices. Meanwhile, in the markets and the shops, the usual articles of food—bread, vegetables, provisions, fresh meat—were being sold in undiminished quantities and at very little above normal prices.

The reasons for this were that the British Navy was keeping our trade routes comparatively clear of hostile ships, and that many cargoes of food bound for Germany were diverted to the United Kingdom Thus, by this one stroke, the position of our enemies was rendered still less favourable, while our own people reaped the benefit. In this fashion was the influence of British sea power doubly demonstrated. It is true that Germany did not depend upon food supplies from oversea to anything like the same extent as Britain: but our enemies were yet to discover that the stoppage of ocean trade was a vital factor in the progress of the war

BRUSSELS IN THE GRIP OF THE INVADING GERMAN.
In the upper picture German soldiers are seen quartered in the Palais de Justice, one of the modern architectural glories of Europe; and in the lower picture, taken from the Hotel de Ville, they are seen in the Grande Place crowding round the army kitchens for their midday meal.

The warfare against commerce began immediately on the declaration of hostilities. Scores of German ships then lying in British harbours were seized by the Customs authorities, and the same fate naturally befell the British ships in German ports. The Declaration of London, which was subsequently adopted, with certain modifications, by the allied Powers as their code of conduct throughout the naval war, lays down that "when a merchant ship belonging to one of the belligerent Powers is at the commencement of hostilities in an enemy port, it is desirable that it should be allowed to depart freely, either immediately, or after a reasonable number of days of grace, and to proceed, after being furnished with a pass, direct to its port of destination, or to any other port indicated to it."

How Germany Attacked Our Commerce

On the day of the declaration of war, the King issued a proclamation stating that, provided our ships were treated equally well in the enemy's ports, German merchantmen would be allowed to leave at any time up to midnight on August 14th—ten days after the declaration. At the same time the Government reserved the right to seize all ships of over 5,000 tons, or having a speed of fourteen knots or above; the obvious reason being that such vessels were capable of being converted into effective commerce raiders after they returned to a German port.

Great hauls of German merchantmen

At sea, the attack upon merchant shipping was prosecuted with vigour, and in this respect we held an enormous advantage over our enemies because of the number of cruisers we had available for such work, and the fact that all ships making for Germany from any country but Sweden, Norway, or Holland, had to make their way past our squadrons in the Channel and the North Sea. Many German ships were captured as they came up the Channel, and others in the attempt to reach their home ports by running round the North of Scotland. Nor was it only in home waters that this war upon German commerce was waged; for when Great Britain went to war the Empire went to war, and at every British port throughout the world where there was a German ship, that ship was detained.

WITH THE KAISER'S HOSTS IN BELGIUM.
A German outpost, in the lower photograph, is waiting not far from the suburbs of Brussels for an expected Belgian attack; and in the upper, some infantry of the German Ninth Army, commanded by General von Boehn, are on the march.

Our cruisers, advised at once by cable and wireless of the outbreak of war, were instantly on the look-out for German ships at sea; but, unfortunately, the success of their activities was largely curtailed by Germany's initiative in forcing war upon us. On August 1st, and possibly even before then, urgent cables were sent from Germany to all the neutral ports used to any great extent by German vessels, ordering that such ships as were there should remain in port, and that all German vessels within wireless range should be advised immediately to return.

By this means the British Navy was robbed of the opportunity of capturing such large ships as the Grosser Kurfürst and the Friedrich der Grosse, of the Norddeutscher Lloyd line, which had just left New York and promptly returned there; while further evidence of Germany's determination to drag this country into the war is provided by the fact that orders were sent at the end of July to many German ships in British ports oversea that they were to make for the nearest neutral port with all possible speed, the object being to prevent their detention by the British authorities.

Even before war was declared, therefore, we had gone far towards driving German commerce off the seas. German liners, food-carrying ships, and tramps, either drew their fires and prepared for an indefinite sojourn in

THE FLOWING TIDE OF RECRUITING.

Upper Picture: A section of the Old Public Schools and University Men's Force at their first parade in Manchester. Five thousand recruits for this force were obtained within ten days. Lower Picture: Recruits for the Seaforth Highlanders, raised by the exertions and financial support of a few prominent Scots in London, leaving the London Scottish headquarters, Buckingham Gate, London, en route for Bedford and war service.

a neutral harbour, or else scurried back in response to the wireless advice to the nearest non-British port. The pressure of British sea-power thus made itself felt before a state of war existed. New York and Boston became crowded with German shipping afraid to venture to sea because of the probability of war and the certainty of British naval predominance.

Just prior to Great Britain's declaration of war, a great deal of interest was aroused by the doings of the Kronprinzessin Cecilie, a 23½-knot 19,500-ton liner belonging to the Norddeutscher Lloyd. This vessel left New York on July 28th, with £2,000,000 in gold, bound for Plymouth, Cherbourg, and Bremen, the gold being consigned to London and Paris. She had almost reached the British Isles when she was informed by wireless of the probable declaration of war between Great Britain and Germany, and she seems at first to have endeavoured to proceed straight to Bremen round the North of Scotland.

Thinking better of this manœuvre, she turned tail and fled at full speed back to America, where she arrived only just in time; for while a state of war existed from midnight on August 4th, the ship arrived at Bar Harbour, off the coast of Maine, at half-past six on the following morning, after an exciting run. Disguised by painting her funnels a different colour, and spreading canvas over her bow and stern, she made for the nearest point at which she could claim the protection of the United States, and she subsequently crept along the American coast to the most convenient harbour.

The escape of the "Gold Ship"

The safe arrival of the ship was not altogether unwelcome in this country, because the delivery of the cargo of gold had been insured principally in the London market, which would have become responsible for payment of the loss if the cargo had been captured. As the gold was consigned to London and Paris, and as there could have been no question of liability to Germany, an enemy Power, such anxiety as was felt in insurance circles in this country was hardly justified. One of the most interesting features in the full-speed run of the Kronprinzessin Cecilie back to America was that a number of American bankers, who happened to be among the passengers, offered to buy the vessel and place her under the American flag. It is to the credit of the German captain that he refused the offer and preferred to take his chance.

Our own merchant shipping at the beginning of the war gave way to a state of temporary panic hardly less complete than that of our enemies. By a stroke of good fortune there happened to be a strike in progress among the engineers of a large section of our merchant shipping, with the result that many vessels which might at the outbreak of war have been in German ports were actually laid up at home, and so were saved to us. Many owners, who had been frightened by " scare " articles, cancelled the sailings of their ships ; but the panic manifested itself most strongly in the insurance market.

The great bulk of British shipping—about four-fifths—was covered by a mutual system of insurance, which provided an indemnity for war risks incurred by ships actually at sea at the outbreak of war, up to the time they reached the nearest British or neutral port. Although this met the interests of the shipowners well enough, it is obvious that it involved a grave danger to the country, inasmuch as it offered a direct inducement to ships to make for the nearest port at the outbreak of war, and to remain there until its close. The insurance rates for covering actual war risks leaped up to an absolutely prohibitive figure, as much as seventy-three guineas per cent. being asked in some cases. The result of this was to close down several routes altogether for a brief period, since voyages could only have been undertaken at serious financial loss.

Effect of exorbitant insurance rates

The first move back to normal conditions was brought about by the scheme of State Insurance for shipping which Mr. Lloyd George announced in the House of Commons on the day of the declaration of war. He pointed out that what was wanted was a scheme to encourage shipping to keep the seas, in order that the supply of food and raw material might be maintained and our trade kept going in war as in peace. It was therefore arranged that, as regards the insurance of the ships themselves, the Government was to fix the premium and to receive eighty per cent. of it, and to assume the responsibility for eighty per cent. of the risk, the remainder being covered by the insurance companies and combinations. The Government also opened an office for the State insurance of cargoes, reserving the right to vary the premiums from a maximum of five guineas to a

IN A STRANGE LAND, BUT CERTAINLY NOT DOWNHEARTED.

British soldiers are comfortable in the midst of discomfort. An alfresco meal, with coal-heaps for background, stone cobbles for tables, sans linen, sans plates, sans almost everything, was all in the day's work to our soldiers in France. The upper photograph shows such a rough-and-ready meal; the lower one, Royal Marine Light Infantry landing at a Continental seaport.

BRITISH AIRSHIP OVER LEICESTER SQUARE, SEPTEMBER 22ND, 1914.

On September 10th, 1914, the Commissioner of Police of the Metropolis advised the public that a British airship would sail over London, and warned inhabitants not to be alarmed at its presence, or fire at it in the mistaken belief that it was hostile. On September 22nd a naval airship sailed round the City of London and the West End, passing over the Admiralty, the War Office, and Buckingham Palace. This drawing, by an eye-witness, represents it as it appeared from Leicester Square.

minimum of one guinea per cent. These arrangements had a vastly reassuring effect on the mercantile community. The terms offered were exceptionally favourable, and indicated the confidence of the Government in the ability of the British Navy to control the trade routes, and to keep them clear of hostile ships. Liners, cargo boats, and tramps began to resume their normal sailings.

Their progress was at first watched with a natural anxiety, because we had received no intimation, either of the hostile forces available for attacking them, or of the plans laid by the Admiralty for checking the schemes of the enemy. Enormously to the surprise of those who had croaked so loudly of risks, it was found that the great majority of our ships not only completed their voyages in safety, but that they crossed thousands of miles of ocean without seeing even a sign of war.

One or two fell in with the enemy, and in South American waters two British ships, the Hyades and the City of Winchester, were sunk soon after the outbreak of hostilities by the German light cruiser Dresden, which was lying in wait on the trade routes north of Pernambuco. In the South Atlantic the British Fleet was represented before the war only by the light cruiser Glasgow, and although she was larger, more powerfully armed, and slightly faster than the German vessel, the task of finding and rounding-up the enemy in such an enormous

BRITISH GIRLS PRESENTING CIGARETTES TO FRENCH SOLDIERS IN PARIS.

A British girl hands cigarettes to French Cuirassiers as they pass through Paris on the way to the front. France possesses twelve regiments of cuirassiers, having steel cuirasses with a brass plate. Germany has an equal number, the cuirass being of white metal. These cuirasses weigh from 13½ to 16 lb. British Life Guards and Royal Horse Guards wear, in peace time, steel cuirasses which cost £3 6s. each. Russia's four regiments of cuirassiers wear cuirasses made of iron and copper, weighing 30 lb.

expanse of ocean was naturally one of infinite difficulty. The crews were taken off the British merchantman before they were sunk; and the loss was somewhat mitigated by the fact that the Hyades, although a British ship, had been chartered by a German firm in Buenos Aires to take a cargo of maize to Germany by Rotterdam.

In the North Atlantic one or two exciting incidents occurred during the early days of the war, but owing to the great superiority of the British and French forces in those waters, things quickly began to resume their normal condition. When war was declared, the Cunard liner Lusitania was lying at New York, and it was reported that the German cruisers Karlsruhe and Strassburg were keeping a discreet eye on the route to Fishguard, in the hope of being able to account for this vessel, which, besides being one of the largest and fastest boats in the British mercantile fleet, was also held at the disposal of the Admiralty for conversion, if need be, into a merchant cruiser.

The British commander-in-chief on the North Atlantic station therefore suggested that the Lusitania should cross under convoy, guarded by one of the cruisers under his command; but there was no cruiser there which had anything like the speed of the Cunarder, whose skipper therefore declined the offer, and determined to trust to his pace. The Lusitania left New York on midnight on August 5th, and, with lights out, proceeded on a course different from that ordinarily followed by Transatlantic shipping. Nevertheless, she was seen and chased by the German cruiser Dresden, which at that time had not proceeded south; but, thanks to her speed, she was able to get safely away. In this she was largely favoured by fortune, for hardly had she successfully shaken off her pursuer, than one of the turbines broke down, and she had to complete the voyage at a speed of under twenty knots.

The Lusitania's fortunate escape

She arrived safely in British waters; but what was intended at the outset to be the quickest run across the Atlantic yet made proved to be the slowest the Lusitania had ever recorded. It was distinctly fortunate that the breakdown in the engine department did not occur while the German cruiser was in sight, for either the Dresden, the Strassburg, or the Karlsruhe could easily have overtaken the great liner at the reduced speed she was forced to adopt.

A similar adventure befell the French liner Lorraine. She also was at New York at the outbreak of war, ready to return to France with four hundred and fifty reservists for the French Army on board. In view of the known presence of German cruisers in the Atlantic, the captain called his officers and crew together and asked them whether they should risk the run across. The reply was an enthusiastic affirmative, and the vessel left New York twelve hours after the Lusitania. Her speed was considerably less than that of the British liner, and things looked unpleasant for her when, on the very evening of her departure, she sighted the Dresden.

There seems little doubt, however, that the German cruiser had consumed too much fuel in her fruitless chase of the Lusitania to be able to pursue the French ship for long, and the Lorraine got safely away. Shortly after escaping this danger the wireless operator on the liner intercepted messages passing between the other German cruisers, from which it was obvious that they were keeping a sharp look-out for her. Here again, however, fortune stepped in. A fog descended on the Atlantic, and with its assistance the Lorraine was enabled to get beyond the possibility of capture, and reached Havre in safety.

The experiences of these vessels, although they came through unscathed, were sufficient to add to the disinclination of shipowners to send their vessels to sea. It goes without saying that there are comparatively few merchant ships with a speed equal even to the twenty-one knots of the Lorraine, and none could reasonably hope for the providential fog which came to the assistance of that ship. The general effect, therefore, might have been serious; but confidence was quickly restored by an announcement made by the Admiralty on August 6th—only two days after the war had begun—to the effect that the whereabouts of all the German cruisers in the Atlantic was known, and that the necessary steps had been taken to deal with them.

A fog that saved a French ship

In point of fact, immediately on the outbreak of war, the Admiralty had greatly increased our cruiser strength in the North Atlantic, and the French forces of the same character had also been considerably strengthened. As Germany was known to have no more than five cruisers in the whole of the Atlantic Ocean—Austria having none—while twenty-four British cruisers were scouring that ocean, it was seen that the risks to shipping were almost negligible. The result was a rapid drop in insurance rates and a corresponding increase in the volume of merchant shipping.

A KIND-HEARTED FRENCH TROOPER ASSISTS HOMELESS PEASANTS.
The plight of many thousands of peaceful French and Belgian peasants, driven from their humble cottages and farms through fear of German brutality, was pitiable in the extreme. This photograph shows a French cavalryman handing a money gift to some ruined peasants who have abandoned their home, and fled with their two small children, rather than face the unknown terrors of a visit from German soldiers.

During the early days of the war we heard, as a matter of fact, very little of the doings of German commerce destroyers, and the first which came into prominence was the Kaiser Wilhelm der Grosse. There was no news of her until she was rounded up and sunk by a British cruiser, but subsequent revelations showed that she had quite an adventurous career before she was sent to the bottom. In normal circumstances she was a vessel belonging to the Norddeutscher Lloyd running between Bremen and New York. Built in 1897, she was six hundred and twenty-six feet long, and displaced 14,349 tons, while her designed speed was twenty-two and a half knots. She was, moreover, one of those vessels which Germany had arranged to take over in the event of war, and to fit out as a commerce destroyer.

Escapades of the Kaiser Wilhelm der Grosse

She was lying at New York at the outbreak of war, preparing to make her ordinary passage across the Atlantic; but as soon as she received the news all her passengers and ordinary cargo were put ashore, and, filling up with coal and stores, she slipped away out of sight. Exactly what her proceedings were will probably never be known. It was practically impossible for her to get into a German port, because as soon as war was declared a cordon of British warships was drawn across the approaches to the German harbours. The next exploit in which she figured

SALUTING THE FLAG OF A FAMOUS FRENCH REGIMENT.

The flag of the Chasseurs-à-pied is decorated with a Roman Eagle, a sergeant of the regiment having captured an Austrian Eagle at the Battle of Solferino on June 24th, 1859. There are thirty battalions of the Chasseurs-à-pied, light infantry, corresponding to the Rifle Corps of the British Army, and their uniform consists of dark-blue tunics and iron-grey trousers.

was the capture of an English fishing vessel, the Tubal Cain, off Iceland. This happened much too soon after her departure from New York to permit of the possibility of her having embarked her armament and ammunition at a German port. Either she carried these accessories on board, or else she shipped them in a neutral port or from a vessel which she met at sea. It is at least certain that she did not return to Germany for them.

Harassing British African trade

In point of fact, there is no reason to doubt that the Kaiser Wilhelm der Grosse had carried her war instructions on board ever since she was first put into service. She had evidently been ordered in certain circumstances to attack British trade on the South African route; for within a few days she was cruising to the south of the Canary Islands. Here she had a merry but a brief existence, though her career was marked throughout by a courtesy which was sadly lacking among the Germans ashore.

On August 14th, the Union Castle liner Galician, homeward bound from the Cape, was approaching the Canaries when she received a wireless message from the British cruiser Carnarvon asking her to state her exact

A LULL IN THE FIGHT AT SOISSONS IN THE GREAT BATTLE OF THE RIVERS.

Soissons, on the River Aisne, saw much of the fiercest fighting during the course of the great battle. Shells from the opposing armies screamed through and over the town, and hand-to-hand conflicts took place in the trenches near by. This picture shows an African Chausseur, two Turcos, and three British soldiers photographed in front of a building that suffered severely from artillery fire.

position. As the captain of the liner had been warned of the possibility of finding hostile ships in his track, he was probably far from displeased to know that a British warship was somewhere in the neighbourhood—at any rate, within wireless call. Everything went well until, shortly after noon on the following day, a large vessel was seen coming up astern. Anxious eyes watched her, but not until the pursuing ship had almost come up with the Galician was it possible to recognise her as the Kaiser Wilhelm der Grosse.

Immediately the wireless operator in the liner began to send out the "S.O.S." message, hoping that the Carnarvon would still be within reach; but hardly had the first letter been clicked out when the German cruiser interrupted with a peremptory: "Send one letter more and I sink you." The Galician was ordered to heave to, and a boat's crew from the Kaiser Wilhelm went aboard. Their first action was to destroy the wireless gear, and then the passengers and crew were drawn up on deck for examination. Two of them turned out to be soldiers returning to England, and these were made prisoners, and instructed to pack their belongings and prepare to return with the Germans.

German Navy men who were gentlemen

To everyone else the boarding party were studiously polite, and rather apologetic for the work they had to do. They requisitioned a quantity of quinine, for which they paid, but they refused to accept a gift of cigars and cigarettes which was pressed upon them, because, as they said, "We should not like it to be said that we robbed the ship." Their examination complete, the Germans went back to the Kaiser Wilhelm with their prisoners, and instructions were given for the Galician to follow closely. This she did all night, the ships steaming in a southerly direction with shrouded lights half through the night the object of the German vessel being to get well off the main trade route. Soon after midnight the cruiser signalled: "Provision all your boats for five days. You will have to abandon your ship."

What this meant everyone knew. They were to be set adrift and left to be picked up by a passing vessel, or to find their way to the nearest coast, while the German cruiser sent the Galician to the bottom. There was no help for it, however, and the work was begun with a will; but within half an hour there came another signal from the Kaiser Wilhelm. "No more orders. You are released. Good-bye!"

THE RIFT OF DAWN IN THE TRENCHES ON THE BATTLE-LINE.

This impressive picture was taken in one of the trenches in France when a sentry stood guard over his fellows who were sleeping after a stiff and exhausting fight on the day before. On this occasion they had been allowed to sleep undisturbed through the night, instead of having the frequent experience of having to rouse themselves and spring to their rifles to make or repel an attack.

C Printed and published by the AMALGAMATED PRESS, LIMITED, The Fleetway House, Farringdon Street, London, E.C.
Published by Gordon & Gotch in Australia and New Zealand; by The Central News Agency, Ltd., in South Africa; by The Standard Literature Co., 13/1, Old Court House Street, Calcutta, and The Imperial News Co., Toronto and Montreal in Canada. *Advertisement applications should be made to The Advertisement Manager, The Fleetway House, Farringdon Street, London, E.C.*

Week ending October 31st, 1914.] [Registered for Canadian Magazine Post.

Part 11. **For Important Notice to Subscribers see overleaf.** **6d. Net.**

The

GREAT·WAR

THE STANDARD HISTORY OF THE ALL-EUROPE CONFLICT

Edited by H·W·Wilson, author of

"With the Flag to Pretoria," "Japan's Fight for Freedom," etc.

Grand Duke Nicholas, Commander-in-Chief of the Russian Armies.

AN ENDURING BINDING FOR AN ENDURING WORK

As THE GREAT WAR begins to grow into a book, the question of binding in enduring form this permanent record of the mighty conflict will occupy the minds of readers.

The publishers are in the position to offer the best possible value in beautiful and durable bindings.

Before the advance in the cost of leather caused by the war, they had the foresight to make an advantageous contract for large supplies at the old price. Readers who buy the publishers' cases will, therefore, get the benefit of this contract, and may congratulate themselves in securing remarkably fine cases at a remarkably low figure. Every 16 parts will constitute a volume, but readers are urged to give an order at once to their newsagent or bookseller for the binding they require. The binding illustrated below is the Half Leather, which combines durability and elegance in a remarkable degree, and is well worth a great deal more than the difference in cost between it and the Cloth. This binding has a full gilt back, while the leather has been dyed a rich scarlet. The sides are reinforced at the corners with specially thick leather covering.

Bound in the publishers' Half Leather cases, the volumes of THE GREAT WAR will enhance the finest library.

The price is but 4/6.

(Turn to page III. of cover.)

PUBLISHERS' HALF-LEATHER BINDING

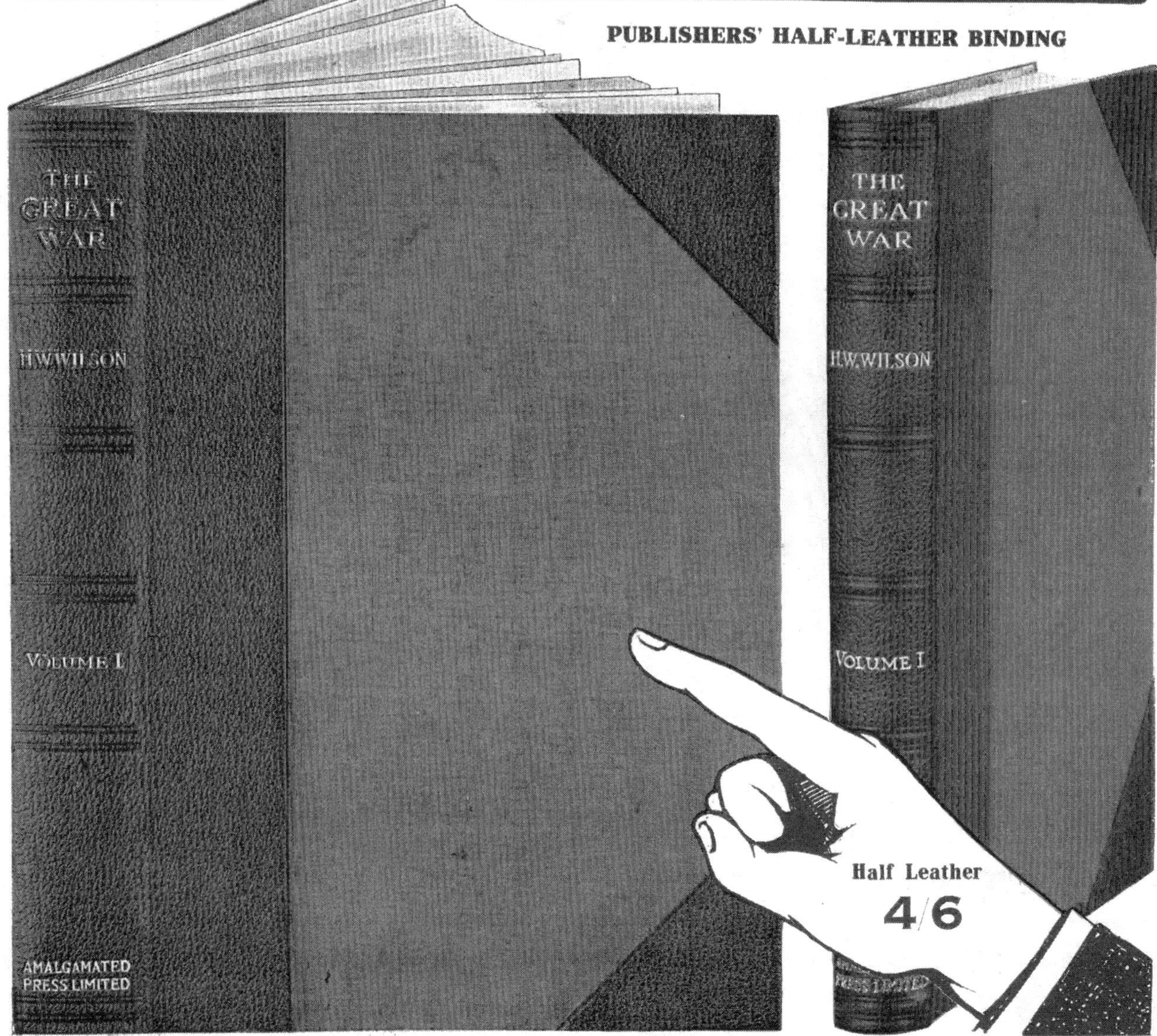

GERMAN "COMMERCE DESTROYER" DESTROYED.

"Bravo, Highflyer!"—In these two words, sent by wireless, the British Admiralty conveyed their congratulations to the British light cruiser Highflyer after the successful attack on the Kaiser Wilhelm der Grosse on August 27th, 1914, off the West Coast of Africa. The photograph shows the German ship, a Norddeutscher Lloyd liner of 14,349 tons, which was converted into a "commerce destroyer" as soon as war was declared, after the Highflyer's guns had finished her career and she was about to disappear for ever beneath the Atlantic waves.

FLOATING DOCK AT TSING-TAU.

Germany expended vast sums on the equipment of Kiao-Chau, her colony in China, of which Tsing-Tau is the port, which Japan began to blockade on August 24th, 1914.

The people on board the Galician, it is hardly necessary to say, were vastly relieved by this sudden change in their prospects, even though at first they could make neither head nor tail of it. The cruiser went off at full speed, and was soon out of sight, while the Galician went about, and resumed her voyage to Teneriffe.

Arriving there two days later she learned that the wireless message which the Kaiser Wilhelm had interrupted with a threat to sink her had just gone far enough to indicate to two of our cruisers in the vicinity that a British ship was in danger somewhere to the south. They had, therefore, set off in that direction, endeavouring to get in touch with the Galician by means of wireless. That ship, of course, did not receive the messages, but they were picked up by the German, who must have come to the conclusion that the British ships were getting too near to be comfortable, and much too near to allow of the people being taken off the Galician prior to that ship being sunk.

Other escapades of the Wilhelm der Grosse

Another British ship, the Arlanza, was also stopped and released by the Kaiser Wilhelm der Grosse, but there were two which did not come so well out of the meeting. On August 16th the New Zealand Shipping Company's steamer Kaipara, from Monte Video, was approaching the Canaries cautiously, having, like the Galician, been warned of possible enemies, when, in the early morning, the Kaiser Wilhelm der Grosse was sighted in chase. As before, an attempt was made to use the wireless apparatus, but again came the threat from the German ship: "If you use your wireless, I will use my guns."

The warning was effective, and the captors proceeded about their business without the least delay. A boat

II

put off, and the Kaipara was boarded. Her wireless was smashed, explosives were placed in the hold, and the crew ordered to take their belongings, get into the boats, and go aboard the Kaiser Wilhelm. When the last man had got aboard the cruiser opened fire. Fifty-three shots were sent into the Kaipara, and at half-past twelve she sank. The captured crew were treated with the utmost courtesy. One of the officers, when he had a chance later on of telling of his experiences, said: " We were provided with some of the saloon berths, and the Germans were most polite to us. It was evident that they did not altogether relish their task. The commander remarked that it was a painful proceeding for him to have to sink our vessel, as it appeared to be wanton destruction of valuable property." However, this did not prevent him from carrying out his orders to the best of his ability, for within a few hours of the sinking of the Kaipara another British ship, the Nyanga, was rounded up and treated in exactly the same fashion. Having accomplished this, the Kaiser Wilhelm der Grosse went into Rio del Oro Bay, in Spanish territory, on the West African coast, where she coaled from a German tramp steamer, the Duala, which had been disguised to represent as closely as possible a Union Castle liner. She then proceeded to sea and cruised about for a week, without, however, doing any further damage, the reason being partly, no doubt, that her exploits had scared British shipping off the route. On August 27th she had again to put into Rio del Oro

Sinking of the Kaipara and Nyanga

SOME INTERESTING UNITS OF THE GERMAN NAVY.
The German gunboat Panther, seen in the top picture, was the ship sent out by the Kaiser to Agadir during the historic dispute about Morocco in July, 1911, and it was erroneously reported sunk in the Mediterranean on August 2nd, 1914. In the middle picture we see the German Dreadnought Helgoland, completed in 1911, a battleship of 21,000 tons displacement and twelve 12 in. guns, and below is the small cruiser Bremen, a 23-knot boat of 3,250 tons, completed in 1904, which proved of some little use to Germany in the early stage of the war in chasing and harassing British merchantmen.

to coal, being met this time by the colliers Magdeburg, Bethania, and Arucas; and it was here that she came to the end of her adventurous career. What happened can best be described in the words of Chief-Officer Wilde, of the Kaipara, who was still a prisoner on board.

" I think it was on the Wednesday, about half-past twelve, while the Kaiser Wilhelm was coaling, that we heard the boatswain piping, and the men rushed up on deck with pistols and bayonets. A petty officer, who spoke English, remarked to me, ' You'll be all right by-and-by. I think it's a British cruiser.' Nothing happened, and coaling was resumed shortly afterwards, the impression being that there had been a false alarm. At two-thirty, however, the captain-lieutenant came to us and said: ' Gentlemen, you will please go to the collier at once. A British cruiser is going to open fire.' We got what clothes we could and jumped aboard the collier Arucas.

The end of a great liner

" Orders were also given to a large number of officers and men of the Kaiser Wilhelm to board the colliers.

THROWING OVERBOARD ALL INFLAMMABLE LUXURIES WHEN A BATTLESHIP IS CLEARED FOR ACTION.

When battleship decks are cleared for action their cabins must be denuded of unnecessary woodwork, lest a hostile shell burst near and start a dangerous fire. From one of the big ships that, early in August, began the blockade of the German North Sea coast, fully one thousand pounds' worth of handsome furniture, including two pianos and an organ, was flung overboard into the North Sea. The officers' quarters principally suffered. To use the phrase of a sailor who assisted at the sacrifice, " It was like throwing a gentleman's drawing-room into the sea."

They did so, and as they jumped from the Kaiser Wilhelm many of them threw their arms into the sea. Suddenly the British cruiser, which proved to be the Highflyer, opened fire, and the Kaiser Wilhelm replied. The Arucas was still made fast to the Kaiser Wilhelm, and the shells whizzed over our heads. The first shot gave us a bit of a shock, but we soon got accustomed to it, and our men conducted themselves with great coolness.

"I took charge of the wheel of the collier for a time, and gradually we moved away from the doomed vessel, which never had a chance against the cruiser, owing to the short range of her guns. We could see the shells from the Kaiser Wilhelm dropping short. One of the Highflyer's first shots disabled the German's port quarter gun and took part of the bridge away. I think the Arucas was about eleven miles away when the Kaiser Wilhelm went down, so that we did not see her sink. Before we had got under way, and while the shells were passing over our heads, some amusement was caused in the Arucas by one of our number impersonating a bookie and asking for bets on the result of the shooting. The Bethania, on board which were a number of the Kaiser Wilhelm's crew, was hit amidships by one of the shells from the Highflyer. The Arucas made for Las Palmas, where we joined the Inanda and sailed for London the same day."

THE MAGDEBURG, A SMALL GERMAN CRUISER
of 4,550 tons, ran ashore at the entrance to the Gulf of Finland on August 27th, 1914, and was blown up by her captain.

THE GERMANIA,
yacht owned by head of the Krupp concern, had come before the war to the Solent and was detained at Southampton by order of the British Prize Court.

The Kaiser Wilhelm was a much heavier vessel than the Highflyer, displacing over 14,000 tons as against the British cruiser's 5,600; but the latter was armed with eleven 6 in. guns as against the German vessel's ten 4·1 in., and had a further advantage in having been built specially for war purposes and in catching the Kaiser Wilhelm at a moment when she was unprepared. Indeed, had the ships met at sea the Highflyer would, in all probability, have failed to account for the German liner, since the latter was appreciably faster and could have shown a clean pair of heels. As it was, however, the Highflyer had rendered excellent service. She had suffered practically no damage herself, and lost only one man killed and five slightly wounded; while she had sent to the bottom the only hostile vessel believed to be at large on that particular trade route.

THE KOENIGSBERG, 3,400-TON GERMAN CRUISER
that attacked and sunk the small British cruiser Pegasus when the latter was at anchor refitting in the harbour of Zanzibar, on September 20th, 1914

The Admiralty sent a congratulatory message to Captain H. T. Buller, of the Highflyer, in which they paid a tribute to the considerate manner in which the men of the lost ship had carried out their work. The message ran: "Bravo! You have rendered a service, not only to Britain but to the peaceful commerce of the world. The German officers and crew appear to have carried out their duties with humanity and restraint, and are therefore worthy of all seamanlike consideration." Prisoners of war would have been perfectly certain of receiving this consideration from British seamen. One of the most

Lowering a boarding boat. The crew are armed with cutlass and pistol. They board suspicious craft and examine papers, holds, and so on.

It takes a matter of two minutes for the boat, which is in charge of a lieutenant-commander, to be lowered and manned.

The boat remains alongside while the officer and part of the crew search the suspected craft.

Finding everything on the foreign trawler satisfactory, the boarding boat returns. These boats include interpreters in their crew.

Morning service on a man-of-war is attended daily by officers and men. The prayers are printed on large cards. Inset: Keeping the sailors fit. They run round the deck, an officer leading the way, every morning after prayers.

WITH A BRITISH CRUISER IN THE NORTH SEA IN WAR TIME

striking effects of the sinking of the Kaiser Wilhelm der Grosse was an immediate drop of twenty-five per cent. in the insurance rates for ships trading to and from South African and South American ports.

An interesting sequel to this action occurred about a fortnight later, when the British warship Vindictive, patrolling the Western Atlantic, took into Kingston, Jamaica, as a prize of war, the Hamburg-Amerika liner Bethania, one of the ships from which the Kaiser Wilhelm had been coaling when she was surprised by the Highflyer. Most of the four hundred men on board proved to have been those who had left the armed ship on the approach of the cruiser (the British soldiers on board the former were, by the way, retaken), and from them it was learned that the Bethania had left Barry on July 10th, arriving at Genoa on the 25th. She left a few days later "for the west coast of South America"; but if that was in reality her intended destination she received wireless orders to modify her programme, and became a floating coal-depot for German commerce marauders.

In laying their plans for a war with Great Britain our enemies had to give much careful consideration to the situation in which they were placed by their lack of coaling stations, and, as we have already seen, an attempt to overcome the difficulty was made by scattering depot ships all over the world. These vessels, which included many luxurious liners belonging to the great German shipping firms, were converted, some of them, into colliers. Some of them also carried stores of food, ammunition, and other things necessary for preserving the fighting efficiency of the German cruisers.

AUSTRIAN SIEGE-GUNS FOR BELGIAN FORTS.

The importance of the thorough conquest of Belgium, from the German point of view, was evidenced by their call upon Austria for assistance when the latter country was being so sorely pressed by the Russians in Galicia. The great siege-gun seen here in its several sections—its motor-tractor (on the right), its gun carriage with recoil apparatus (in the centre waggon), and the gun itself (on the left)—is a formidable engine of war, which is fortunately not easily mobile, and is therefore almost impossible for use in field work. The upper picture shows the gun without its mounting, and a number of Austrian officers.

Every ship was given a settled programme, which was not to be deviated from except under pressure of superior force. Definite arrangements were made whereby a certain cruiser would be met at a certain place on a certain date by a ship carrying stores; and when the store-ships had exhausted their supplies they could return to a neutral port to replenish them, provided always that they were able to elude the British and French ships on the look-out for them. In the early stages of the war this plan was carried out with considerable success, although from the beginning it was clearly only a matter of time before the overwhelming superiority of the Franco-British naval forces would wear down and wipe

THE AUSTRIAN BATTLESHIP ZRINYI

of 14,500 tons, completed in 1911. The British and French naval strength in the Mediterranean prevented the Austrian Fleet from taking any aggressive part in the early stage of the war.

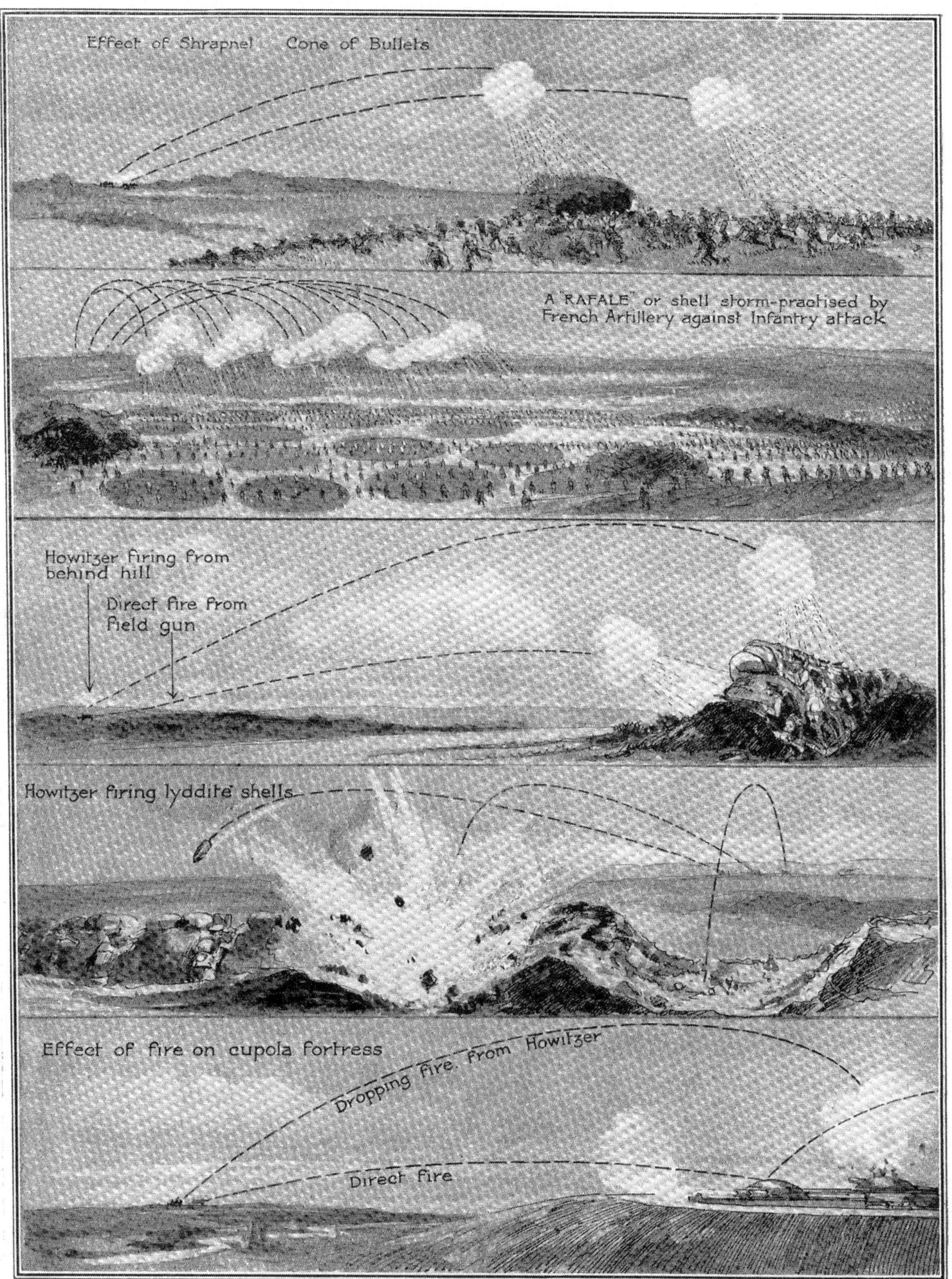

THE VARIOUS KINDS OF GUN-FIRE EMPLOYED IN MODERN ARTILLERY PRACTICE.

First diagram: Shrapnel-fire on advancing infantry. The shells are timed to explode, when once the range is found, at a certain distance; it is unnecessary for them to hit an object. Second diagram: Shell-storm practised by French artillery. Fired at a high angle, the shells burst in mid-air over the advancing troops. Third diagram: A comparison between the effects of howitzer and field-gun fire on men in trenches. The howitzer fires at a high angle from behind a covering hill and drops its shell into the trenches; the field gun, in the open, fires direct, and its shell bursts in front of the sandbags, and is therefore practically harmless. Fourth diagram: Howitzers firing against entrenchments high-explosive shells which burst only on contact. When a lyddite shell does hit its object the result is a terrific explosion. Great cavities are made in the ground, and for hundreds of yards round the actual point of contact the tremendous shock is felt. Fifth diagram: Howitzer and field-gun fire on a cupola fortress. Howitzers are the only effective weapons against such fortresses; howitzer shells drop on to the iron covering of the cupola and reduce it to scrap iron. The field gun fires direct, and if it strikes the cupola the projectile simply delivers a glancing blow and rebounds.

out every German ship on the seas The fate of the Kaiser Wilhelm der Grosse and the Bethania are instances of what was to be expected, not all at once, but ultimately.

A similar position arose on one occasion early in the war in the Western Atlantic. On August 7th the armoured cruiser Suffolk discovered the German light cruiser Karlsruhe coaling at sea from the Norddeutscher Lloyd liner Kronprinz Wilhelm. Unfortunately, the German ship had ample warning of the Suffolk's approach, and, having a greater superiority in speed (she was designed for twenty-eight knots as against the British ship's twenty-three), was able to slip away. The Suffolk at once sent a wireless message to the Berwick and the Bristol, which joined her in the chase. The Berwick, however, was no faster than the Suffolk, but the Bristol, a twenty-five knot ship, began to draw ahead of them.

Escape by reason of higher speed

The Karlsruhe was considerably faster than the Bristol, but as the latter got further and further away from her consorts the German ship began to hang back, as though prepared to engage the Bristol in single combat. Night was beginning to fall, and the sea was rough, making accurate shooting almost impossible. Nevertheless, these two cruisers fought for half an hour, and although the Bristol was not hit once she claimed to have put several shells into the German. Then, however, the Suffolk and Berwick came rapidly up, and the Karlsruhe again put on speed and ran. The Bristol fired at the retreating ship with her forward 6 in. gun as long as she was within range, and when the Karlsruhe took refuge later in the neutral port of San Juan, Porto Rico, it was stated that her stern was riddled with shell, and that she had one of her after guns smashed, and eight men injured.

This was only one of the many incidents during the war which brought home the disadvantages under which our ships laboured through their inability to outreach German ships in speed. It is certain that the whole of the German ships operating on the high seas would have been hunted down and sunk much more quickly than was actually the case if we had advanced step by step with Germany as she increased the speed of her cruisers.

Other German ships carrying supplies for the commerce raiders were captured or sunk in various places; but, apart from armed merchantmen, not a single German cruiser outside European waters was accounted for during the first seven weeks of the war. Nevertheless, the damage they did was infinitesimal, and by the middle of September only twelve British ships had been sunk at sea. On the other hand, German commercial shipping was everywhere held up. Only in very few cases was it necessary for a British warship to sink a vessel, as there was nearly always a British port close handy into which the ship could be sent as a prize, a facility Germany did not enjoy.

FROM BERLIN FOR THE EASTERN FRONTIER.

The Russian raid into East Prussia in August, 1914, caused the Kaiser's war lords to dispatch large bodies of troops eastwards in haste. The trains were crowded, and soldiers packed like sardines had to ride even in the engine-tenders and on top of the coal supply.

RUSSIAN CAVALRY REVIEW BY THE TSAR.

CHAPTER XVI.

RUSSIA'S STUPENDOUS TASK AND HER STUPENDOUS ARMY.

German High Policy—Origin of the Triple Alliance—The Dual Alliance—The German Problem of the War on Two Fronts—Kuropatkin's Work for Russia—Vast Extent of Russia's Dominions and the Difficulty of Attacking Her—The Country and Fortresses of East Prussia—The Military Value of German and Austrian Railways—Russia's Power of Defence and Attack—Germany's Naval Supremacy in the Baltic—System of Russian Conscription—Russia's Fighting Strength—Quality of the Russian Soldier—Russia's Military Leaders—The Tsar's Pledge to Poland.

THE German Empire, proclaimed in the old palace of the French Kings at Versailles in January, 1871, inherited the tradition of Prussian diplomacy, and a cardinal point in that tradition was friendship with Russia. To his dying day the aged Emperor William I. clung to this ideal, and as he lay on his death-bed almost his last word to his son and successor was a recommendation to "cultivate the friendship of the Tsar."

But even before Kaiser William I. passed away on March 9th, 1888, German policy had taken a new departure. The old Emperor had long ceased to be entirely master in his own house, and the direction of affairs was largely controlled by the arbitrary will of Prince Bismarck. At the Congress of Berlin, in 1878, the German Chancellor had sided with Lord Salisbury in opposing Russia's claim to parcel out the Balkan lands at her own good pleasure after the war with Turkey. Bismarck at the time protested that he was the best of friends to the Tsar, and that he was acting as "an honest broker" in effecting a compromise between the rival ambitions of Austria and Russia in the Balkan Peninsula in the interest of a lasting peace. But it was the beginning of a gradual drifting apart of the two neighbours who had so long been friends, and often allies. Within a twelvemonth of the Berlin Congress a treaty of alliance was signed between Germany and Austria. It was not published till nine years later, but, long before its publication, it was a secret known to half the world. The alliance was represented as a league of peace intended to prevent any disturbance of the existing state of affairs, either on the Danube or the Rhine, by Russian ambitions in the Balkan lands or the French longing for a reconquest of Alsace-Lorraine. Italy joined the league in 1886, and it thus became the Triple Alliance.

M. SERGIUS SAZONOFF,
the Russian Foreign Minister, who played a great part in determining the policy of Russia during the last days of July, 1914. A dignified speaker, after the manner of Lord Lansdowne, he was formerly secretary to the Russian Embassy in London.

The treaty with Austria had no sooner been signed than Germany began quietly and unobtrusively to fortify her eastern frontier and develop her railway system in Pomerania, East Prussia, and the province of Posen. Russia replied by a gradual change in the peace stations of her Army, so as to keep the greater part of it permanently in garrisons and fortresses between Moscow and the Austro-German border. At the same time the relations between St. Petersburg and Paris became more and more friendly, and an *entente* developed into an alliance between France and Russia.

Long before this new treaty had been actually signed German statesmen and soldiers had recognised the practical certainty

KK

RUSSIANS RIDE TO BATTLE WITH MUSIC AND SONG.
Many of the Russian regiments have vocal and instrumental orchestras that accompany the troops to battle in place of the regimental bands. The singers are specially trained, and with cymbals, bells, and other hand instruments accompany the martial and national songs they sing while marching along. The effect of this is most inspiring, and raises the ardour of the soldiers to a pitch that the music of an ordinary regimental band could not do.

that, in case of war with France on the Rhine, Russia would take the field as her ally. In German military literature of the last twenty-five years the problem of "the war on two fronts" is a frequent topic of debate. Germany realised that she must be ready to meet both a French advance towards the Rhine and a Russian march across the Vistula, in the event of her being involved in war with either of her neighbours. The accepted German theory of defence against this double attack was that the mobilisation and concentration of the Russian armies would lag behind that of the French; that this would enable the main force of the German armies to be flung against France, with a fair prospect that a decisive battle would be fought on that side before the Russian pressure on the eastern frontier could become serious, and that the defence of this frontier might at the outset be safely entrusted to a small part of the German first-line troops, backed by Landwehr forces, and supported by the main mass of the Austrian Army.

The alliance with Italy was relied upon to remove all anxiety as to a hostile movement on the Italian frontiers of Austria, and to divert from the main front of operations in the west a portion of the French Army, which would be required to meet an Italian attack on the line of the Alps and along the Riviera.

In Russia there is less open discussion of military possibilities than in other countries. But we know something of the anticipations of the Russian Staff as to conflict with Germany and Austria from a remarkable document summarised by General Kuropatkin in his work, "The Russian Army and the Japanese War," published in 1909.

Kuropatkin's work for Russia

Kuropatkin was appointed Minister of War at St. Petersburg in 1898, and held that post until February, 1904, when he left Europe to take command of the Russian armies in the Far East against the Japanese. His first act as Minister of War was to arrange for the drawing up of an elaborate report on the condition of the Russian Army, and the defence of the various frontiers of the Empire, as well as on the opportunities existing in these regions for a counter-attack.

Among the passages from this report embodied in his book there is a very full summary of his views as to the possibilities of military action on the Austro-German frontiers. These are of special interest now that

Russia has had to put forth her strength in this very direction.

Here in Great Britain it has been the fashion to speak as if an attack on this eastern frontier of the Central European Powers would be a comparatively easy matter for the huge armies of the Tsar. The "Russian steam-roller" has become a favourite phrase of the journalists, a popular suggestion of a huge moving mass crushing down every obstacle to its advance.

But Kuropatkin, in his official report from the War Ministry, dated 1900, frankly recognises that the obstacles on this western frontier of Russia are of the most serious character, and speaks of the failure of a Russian advance upon it as quite possible. He had no illusions as to the difficulties of the task that would be imposed upon an army operating in this direction.

THE WONDERFUL HORSE OF THE WONDERFUL COSSACK.
More than half the reputation of the Cossack should be credited to his horse, a small animal, short of limb and neck, but a wonderful stayer, thriving on poor food, docile, intelligent, indifferent to weather and ignorant of the luxury of a stable. On forced marches he can carry three men, one on each stirrup and one in the saddle, as seen in the picture.

To understand the conditions of the military problem, and to follow with intelligent interest the record of the campaign in Eastern Europe, one must have some clear ideas about the forces that Russia could place in the field, and the character of the region in which they had to operate. Everyone knows that Russia is beyond all comparison the most extensive State in Europe, but few realise the enormous size of her territory. When a traveller from England on his way to Moscow reaches the frontier station at Wirballen he feels he is nearing his journey's end, for at last he is on Russian ground. But he is still actually nearer his starting point on the Continent at Ostend than he is to Moscow, and when he reaches that city he is still only half way across European Russia. Once only in the whole course of history has a western conqueror marched into the heart of Russia and seized the Holy City of Moscow. That was when Napoleon dated his bulletin of victory from the Kremlin in 1812, and his success, such as it was, proved his ruin.

Great extent of Russian territory

Her vast extent, and the ease with which wide tracts of country can be laid waste before an advancing enemy by the mere firing of wooden villages and barns, still make Russia secure against any far-reaching scheme of foreign invasion. Only her coasts and her frontier provinces are open to attack.

The Russian land frontier towards Austria and Germany is 1,500 miles long. The greater part of this extended line is the frontier of Russian Poland. The province projects westward from the main mass of the Russian territory, like a huge bastion wedged in between German lands on the north and west and Austrian

OFFICERS IN THE RUSSIAN ARMY AT RELIGIOUS SERVICE IN A PUBLIC SQUARE BEFORE GOING TO WAR.
The soul of Russia was stirred to its depths by the attempts to bring the southern Slavs under the heel of the Germanic Empires, and every man in the Russian armies entered the campaign fired by religious zeal, taking up his weapons as a holy duty. The ceremony photographed here was most impressive, with all the dignity and solemnity of a sacrament.

on the south. A glance at a map of Europe will show that the Austrian province of Bohemia projects in much the same way into the lands of the German Empire. But Bohemia is a bastion ramparted with mountain walls. Russian Poland is a bastion merely marked out upon the ground without any natural barrier on any one of its three fronts. The line that divides Russia from her neighbours on this side is a purely artificial one, defined only by the posts set up at intervals along it for custom-house purposes. It is a political, not a natural frontier, marked out in somewhat arbitrary fashion when, after the turmoil of the Napoleonic wars, the map of Europe was being resettled at the Congress of Vienna.

ONE OF THE DREADED COSSACKS.

This Russian province and the adjacent borderlands are part of the great plain that, beginning in Northern Germany, stretches across European Russia to the Ural Mountains. Only on the south side of the Polish plain is there any high ground. Here the Austrian province is a sloping terrace at the base of the Carpathian Mountains, which divide these northern lowlands from the raised plain of Hungary.

Compared with the giant Alpine ranges, the Carpathians are hills rather than mountains. Along this Galician border they form a broad belt of forest-clad sandstone ridges, mostly under 5,000 feet high, traversed by a number of passes and hill roads, forming an admirable natural defence for Hungary. The

RUSSIAN PRIESTS BLESS THE ARMIES ABOUT TO MARCH TO THE FRONT.
Russians are much more given to the expression of religious feeling than the more reserved nations of the west, and a war sanctified by the approval of the Church in addition to being in accord with national sentiment is essentially a people's war. The blessing of the Church is a ceremony that lends the Russian soldier the zeal of a fanatic, and all history shows that such zeal gives a formidable strength to an army.

AUSTRALASIA
ANSWERS THE CALL OF EMPIRE

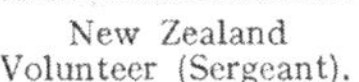
New Zealand Volunteer (Sergeant).

AUSTRALIAN CADETS INSPECTED BY LORD KITCHENER AT BISLEY.

New Zealand Volunteer (Private).

THE AUSTRALIAN LIGHT HORSE.

GROUP OF AUSTRALIAN OFFICERS.

THE VICTORIA LIGHT HORSE AT KILMORE, NORTH OF MELBOURNE.

LL

The King's Message to his great Oversea Dominions on September 10th 1914 contained these words:

"Paramount regard for treaty faith and the pledged word of rulers and peoples is the common heritage of Great Britain and of the Empire. My peoples in the Self-Governing Dominions have shown beyond all doubt that they wholeheartedly endorse the grave decision which it was necessary to take."

The endorsement took the practical form of ships, men, and money. The spontaneity and the enthusiasm displayed by the citizens of the Oversea Dominions in the cause of treaty rights, national honour, and Imperial defence soon showed that behind the fighting-line there stood solid the great Empire scattered throughout the seven seas.

Australia and New Zealand, in addition to raising contingents for assistance in Europe, took strong action in their own part of the world. On August 29th a force from New Zealand occupied German Samoa, and on September 25th Australians announced their occupation of the seat of government of Kaiser Wilhelm Land, in German New Guinea.

OFFICERS AND MEN OF THE AUSTRALIA.
The Australia is a sister ship of the Indefatigable and New Zealand, with a displacement of 19,200 tons and a speed of twenty-six knots.

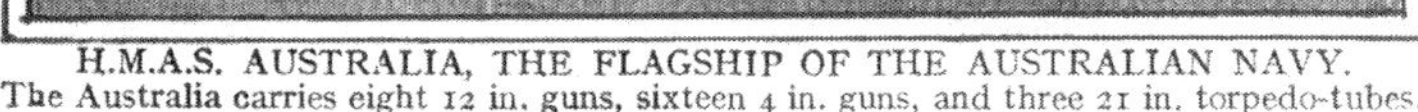

H.M.A.S. AUSTRALIA, THE FLAGSHIP OF THE AUSTRALIAN NAVY.
The Australia carries eight 12 in. guns, sixteen 4 in. guns, and three 21 in. torpedo-tubes. Her commander is Rear-Admiral Sir George Edwin Patey, seen above.

From the painting by]

H.M.A.S. MELBOURNE.

THE 23RD ARMY MEDICAL CORPS OF THE 6TH MILITARY DISTRICT—TASMANIA.
In 1911 the Australian Government adopted a defence scheme based on Lord Kitchener's recommendations.

AUSTRALIA AND NEW ZEALAND LEND THEIR WELCOME AID IN THE GREAT IMPERIAL CAUSE.

FLEET OF THE AUSTRALIAN COMMONWEALTH AT SEA.
Together with its flagship the battle-cruiser Australia, the Australian Navy includes the protected cruisers Melbourne, Sydney, and Brisbane, and six destroyers.

THE CREW OF THE AUSTRALIA.
The complement of the Australia consists of eight hundred officers and crew, and her commander is Admiral of the Australian Fleet.

[A. J. W. Burgess.

H.M.S. NEW ZEALAND, A BATTLE-CRUISER OF THE BRITISH GRAND FLEET.
A sister ship of the Australia, the New Zealand was provided by the Government of the island Dominion. The portrait is that of Captain Lionel Halsey, her commander.

PARADE OF AUSTRALIAN TROOPS IN MELBOURNE BEFORE THE WAR.
Military conscription prevails in Australia and the total strength of all classes of military service is almost 200,000 men.

RUSSIAN COSSACKS CHARGE THE GERMAN DEATH'S HEAD HUSSARS IN EAST PRUSSIA, AUGUST 26th, 1914.

On the evening of August 26th, 1914, Mr. R. W. Ames, the British manager of a large estate in East Prussia, witnessed through his field-glasses a battle between 10,000 Germans and 15,000 Russians at a place named Schwansfeld, between Korschen and Bartenstein. The Cossack cavalry charged the German Death's Head Hussars full tilt. There was a tremendous impact, and hand-to-hand fighting, and then, all of a sudden, the whole German line began with one accord to retreat. Towards Bartenstein the German cavalry fled, with the Cossacks pursuing and killing them in large numbers. At the same battle Russian infantry, after an artillery bombardment, charged with the bayonet and cut the Germans up in small parties. This picture was drawn from a personal description given to the artist by Mr. Ames.

province of Galicia, the Polish territory of the Austrian Empire, lies outside this natural rampart, and is thus a terraced slope descending to the northern plain that stretches from its margin to the shores of the Baltic.

Across the plain winds the broad, sluggish stream of the Vistula. The great river is to this eastern land what the Rhine is to Western Europe. Frozen or encumbered with drift ice in the winter months, it is during the rest of the year a main highway of traffic, navigable for the greater part of its course, and bearing on its waters huge rafts of timber from the forests, and scores of steamers with strings of lumbering barges trailing astern of them. On its banks, in the midst of the plain, stands Warsaw, the old capital of Poland, and now the political, military, and business centre of the Russian province.

Russia's natural and political frontiers

There is only one other large town in Russian Poland—Lodz, not long ago a country village, but now a busy industrial centre, with its high-street six miles long, and right and left of it in short side streets tall factory buildings. This paucity of large towns is characteristic, not only of Russian Poland, but of the whole Empire. The last census shows that in European Russia there are only twenty-four places that claim a population of over a hundred thousand. Russia is a country of agricultural villages. There are more than 150,000 of them between the Vistula and the Ural.

The plain of the Vistula is not an absolute dead level, but there is nothing that can be called a hill. The ground undulates in long, flat-topped waves, and in the hollows run the many tributary streams and lesser rivers

TYPE OF RUSSIAN HOWITZER AT PRACTICE FIRING.
Russian experience in her great war with Japan taught the Tsar's military advisers some lessons which, though bitter, were profitable, and one direct result was a great improvement in the Russian artillery arm, both in the guns themselves and in the gun practice.

that feed the great waterway—streams as sluggish as the Vistula itself, and often with low, marshy banks that are flooded in the time of rains. There are wide stretches of woodlands, the refuge of the insurgent bands in the Polish risings of 1830 and 1863. Between the woods are open lands with many villages, rich lands with a deep soil, somewhat primitively tilled.

The northern part of this plain of the Vistula belongs to Prussia Here the lands of the German Empire interpose between Russian Poland and the Baltic. The border district between the Narev River and the frontier line is a region of marshy forests; then inside the German frontier line is the region of the Masurian Lakes. This is a land of innumerable lakes and pools, with belts and clumps of fir and beech woods, occupying much of the land between their swampy margins. In the clearings by the lakes and in the woodlands there are the red-walled villages, for there is plenty of clay for brick-making In fact, the clayey soil accounts for the abundance of lakes and pools.

The marsh lands of East Prussia

Beyond this wilderness of lake and wood there is a slight rise of the ground along the Baltic shore between the low-lying delta of the Vistula and the mouth of the River Pregel. This belt of higher and firmer land was in old times the main highway between Northern Germany and Muscovy. The great lagoon of the Frisches Haff lies

THE GREAT WAVE OF RUSSIA'S MANHOOD BEGINS TO ROLL WESTWARD.
The mobilisation of the Russian armies was rapid beyond all expectation, and Russia was able to press over Germany's eastern frontier and cause an easing of the pressure of German activity in Northern France much sooner than Germany had thought possible.

between the river mouths, and at each end of it is a famous city. Dantzic, on the Vistula delta, is a great port, once a city of the famous Hansa League of trading republics, later the chief port of Poland, now Germany's main trading post on the Baltic—a city that keeps much of its old-world look, thanks to the quaint gabled houses, built centuries ago, in its narrow streets. By the branches of the Vistula and the land-locked expanse of the Frisches Haff, Dantzic has a safe inner waterway to the Pregel where by the river mouth stands old Königsberg, once a mere blockhouse fort of the Teutonic knights against the wild Slavs to the eastward, now a fortress of the Prussian kingdom, whose history is closely linked with that of Königsberg (" the King's Hill "), the place where the Prussian kings were crowned.

German citadels in East Prussia

Dantzic and Königsberg together form the citadel of Germanic power in this Baltic coast region. Königsberg is surrounded with a circle of strong forts, and further guarded by the inundations fed by the stream of the Pregel. Its communications with Dantzic along the Frisches Haff are guarded by the batteries of Pillau, at the entrance of the great sea lagoon. Dantzic has its bastioned ramparts and outlying forts, and to the seaward is protected by the new fortress of Weichselmünde (" the Vistula mouths "). The road and railway crossings of the Vistula delta are guarded by the fortified towns of Dirschau and Marienburg, and on this side much of the flat land can be easily laid under water. Along its lower course the Vistula is a German river. Where it leaves Russian Poland it is guarded by the first-class fortress of Thorn. Here the far-flung circle of strong forts covers a great railway junction. Half-way between Thorn and the fortifications of Dantzic and the delta is the fortress of Graudenz.

This fortified line of the Vistula, with the advanced post of Königsberg, forms the armed barrier of East Prussia. In front of the line the country is difficult for an invader in an autumn campaign. Behind the Masurian Lakes and woods a level plain extends towards the lower Vistula. It is a region famous in history as the scene of Napoleon's victories at Eylau and Friedland. The story of that campaign tells how, when the autumn rains were followed by alternate frost and thaw, the country became a quagmire. Any movement of troops was impossible. It became difficult even to feed the armies, for the transport waggons sank to their axle-trees in mud, and had to be abandoned.

THE TSAR INSPECTING THE RUSSIAN RED CROSS.
Accompanied by Red Cross nurses, the Tsar is here seen inspecting hospital workers before they left for the German frontier. The picture above shows Russian infantry marching along the railway line.

A SWIFT CHARGE BY A DETACHMENT OF RUSSIAN CAVALRY.
A snapshot, taken at the Russian military manœuvres, showing a troop of cavalry taking up a position. No army in recent years has made such progress as the Russian, and none has troops of better fighting quality.

Thorn belongs both to the northern chain of defences and to those of the German centre facing Russian Poland. The line is prolonged southward by the great fortress of Posen, and the fortified places of Glogau, Breslau, and Neisse in Silesia. Austria supplies the right of the great semicircle of fortresses. The citadels of her defence of Galicia are Cracow and Przemysl. The former was once the second city of the old Polish kingdom. The latter is a purely military post, with practically no civilian population. It is a village converted into a fortress.

This chain of fortresses, extending over a front of over a thousand miles, is not, however, the only defence of the frontier. Within the last few years a number of positions have been prepared for defence by entrenchments between these permanent works, and even more important from a military point of view has been the development of the railway system. The time is long past when soldiers regarded a mere line of fortresses as constituting a safe protection for a frontier. Passive defence is doomed to eventual failure, and counter-attack is the best means of beating off an assailant. A blow is better than a parry. And a well-developed railway system along a frontier, and immediately in rear of it, makes it possible for the defence to concentrate rapidly a striking force on any desired point.

Military importance of railways

General Kuropatkin, in his report on the military situation on the Russo-Polish frontier, dwelt upon the admirably-developed railway system of Germany and Austria as the chief factor of its strength. He compared it with the backward railway system of Russia in order to bring out clearly the advantage that Russia's possible enemies would possess in a war on this border of the Tsar's Empire. Since he wrote, in 1900, something has been done by Russia to improve the railways of the Polish frontier land, but the Germans and Austrians have been busy in the same direction, and most of what he wrote still holds good.

We shall see, in the German defence of East Prussia, what effective use was made in at least one instance of the railway system which Kuropatkin thus described. If he overestimated the force Germany could move to the front at the outset, this was because he purposely left out of account the detaining effect of the French alliance in a study of Russia's own resources for defence and attack. He thus summed up the situation:

TROOPS OF THE TSAR PHOTOGRAPHED IN GALICIA.
This photograph, which reached London via Stockholm, shows a detachment of the Russian army that operated in the Lemberg district of Galicia. The upper photograph, taken in Russia, illustrates a Russian army motor squadron before leaving for the scene of war.

"By the expenditure of vast sums of money, Germany has made ready in the most comprehensive sense to march rapidly across our borders with an army of one million men. She has seventeen lines of railway (twenty-three tracks) leading to our frontiers, which would enable her to send to the front more than five hundred troop trains daily. She can concentrate the greater part of her armed forces on our frontier within a few days of the declaration of war; while, apart from this question of speedy mobilisation, she has at her command far greater technical resources, such as light railways, artillery, ordnance, and engineering stores, particularly for telegraphs, mobile siege parks, etc., than we have. She has also made most careful preparation for a determined defence of her own border provinces, especially those of Eastern Prussia.

German war preparations on her eastern border

"The first-class fortresses of Thorn, Königsberg, and Posen are improved yearly, entrenched camps are built at the most important junctions, and material lies ready stacked for the rapid semi-permanent fortification of field positions. The crossing places on the Vistula have been rapidly placed in a state of defence, as have also the various towns and large villages. The whole population, indeed, is making ready for a national struggle.

"In the matter of railway development the Austrians have also left us far behind. While they, by means of eight lines of rail (ten tracks), can run two hundred and sixty trains up to the frontier every twenty-four hours, we can only convey troops up to the same point on four lines. As any of their troops on the frontier would be in advance of the Carpathians, this range was formerly looked upon as an obstacle to retirement, and to communication between Galicia and the rest of Austria. But in the last ten years it has been pierced by five lines of railway, and preparations have been made to lay three more."

THE "LITTLE FATHER" OF ALL THE RUSSIAS INSPECTING ONE OF HIS REGIMENTS.
It is commonly believed that the Russian Army is a host of giants. As a matter of fact, the average Russian soldier is shorter than our own, five feet four probably being a generous allowance of height for the whole army; five feet being the infantry minimum, and five feet three that of the cavalry. The Russian soldier, however, is more thickly built and heavier and slower than our own. Seventy per cent. of Russian conscripts cannot read or write when they join the army.

The railways running directly to the frontiers are linked up by cross lines, facilitating the movement of troops along the wide curve from Przemysl to Dantzic and Königsberg. It must be noted that the extreme east of Galicia is left out of this scheme of combined railway and fortress defence. Even the great city of Lemberg was not permanently fortified.

Thus organised, this Austro-German frontier line, by its very configuration, offers striking advantages both for attack and defence. For the former there is the possibility of a converging march into Russian Poland. For the latter there is the advantage to the defending forces that whatever front of advance the Russians may select for their main attack they must at least provide a covering force to face the other two fronts of the encircling frontier. And defeat on either of these would bring the advance upon the selected point of attack to a standstill.

Russian provision against counter-attack

Let us now see how Russia provided both for the defence of the Polish province and for a counter-attack against Austria and Germany.

Eastward of the Polish plain lies the wide region of marsh and pool traversed by the River Pripet and its numerous tributary streams. The "marshes of Pinsk" (or, to give them their alternative name, the "marshes of the Pripet") extend over an area of some 300,000 square miles. Drainage works on a large scale were begun about 1894, and canals were being made through the marsh lands, with the result that portions of the district have been reclaimed, but even though railways have been carried across the district, the marshes still formed

THE GRAND DUKE NICHOLAS,
Commander-in-Chief of the Russian Armies.

GENERAL BRUSSILOFF.
Decorated by the Tsar for his masterly generalship at Kalitz.

GENERAL SUKHOMLINOFF,
the Russian Minister of War.

NICHOLAS II., EMPEROR OF ALL THE RUSSIAS,
Supreme Commander-in-Chief of the World's Greatest Army.

GENERAL SAMSONOFF,
the brilliant Russian General who fell at Osterode, in East Prussia, on August 31st, 1914.

GENERAL RUSSKY,
who captured Lemberg, the capital of Galicia, from the Austrians on September 2nd, 1914.

GENERAL RENNENKAMPF,
the leader of the brilliant raid into East Prussia in the early weeks of the war.

a region in which no army could operate, and they were thus a barrier dividing Western Russia into two separate theatres of war, the northern and the southern. South of the marshes the belt of territory by which the railways and roads from Southern Russia enter Poland is guarded by a group of three fortresses—Dubno, Rovno, and Lusk. West of the marshes, in the Polish plain itself, there is a still larger group of fortresses that forms the citadel of the Russian power in this direction, and the advanced base of operations against Germany and Austria.

The great fortresses of Poland

These fortresses are Warsaw, Ivangorod, and Brest Litowski. Until after the rising of 1863, Warsaw was the only fortress in Poland, and its citadel was chiefly intended to serve as the stronghold of the garrison that overawed the Polish capital. When the Russian Staff took in hand the reorganisation of the frontier defences on a large plan, Warsaw was converted into a modern fortress with its girdle of advanced forts, and purely military stations of the same type of fortification were erected at Ivangorod and Brest, with a third fortress—Novo Georgievsk—a few miles north-west of Warsaw, at the confluence of the Vistula and its chief tributary the Narev.

The three fortresses and Warsaw are sometimes spoken of as the "Polish quadrilateral." A more correctly descriptive name for the group is "the Polish triangle," for Novo Georgievsk is really an outpost of Warsaw and the first of the line of fortified posts that guard the crossings of the River Narev. The fortresses of the "triangle," linked together by railway lines and good

A RUSSIAN REGIMENT AT DIVINE SERVICE: THE TSAR AT A HOSPITAL.
Officers and men of the Preobrejensky Regiment at a religious service held prior to their departure for the front. The Russian soldiers, regarding the great conflict as a holy war, had no fear of death while taking part in it. Each company has its song-leader, who marches in front and "gives out the hymns," receiving special pay. Inset: The Tsar, with nurses and soldiers, at a Petrograd hospital.

A SCENE IN THE RUSSIAN MOBILISATION.

The countries of Western Europe consist largely of cities. Russia, on the other hand, is a country of villages—there are more than 150,000 in European Russia alone—and these were called upon to give up their manhood for holy war against Teuton aggression. The lower picture shows the Holy Tree of Maria Remele, near Budapest, hung with ikons of the Orthodox Greek Church by the quaking inhabitants of the district to propitiate the Russian hordes.

roads, and at the apex of the whole Russian railway system towards the west, form a fortified region, the citadel of the Russian power on its Austro-German frontier. Two of the fronts look towards Germany, the third towards Austria, thus presenting a line of defence towards each section of the enemy's frontiers.

But the purpose of this vast entrenched camp is not entirely or even primarily defensive. It is the fortified base of operations for the army of Russian Poland. Within the triangle huge accumulations of supplies of every kind have been gradually collected, and the railways are provided with extensive sidings and long detraining platforms at the stations. Russia, too, recognises that attack is the best form of defence.

Defences for lines of communication

To guard the communications of the fortified "triangle" with Northern Russia, and to protect the country north of the Pripet region from a German invasion from East Prussia, the line of the Narev, east of the frontier forest lands, has been selected for defence. The marshy banks of the river render it difficult to cross except at certain well-known points. At these every bridge is covered by fortifications. These permanently-protected river crossings are at Novo Georgievsk, Zegrje, Pultusk, Rozan, and Ostrolenka. The line of defence is prolonged north-eastward by the fortified towns of Lomza, Ossovetz, Bielostok, Grodno, and Kovno, the last two on the Niemen.

This line of fortified positions not only secures the crossings of an unbroken series of waterways, marking out a line of defence against East Prussia, but also covers two lines of railways running from the north-east into Russian Poland. These protected railways enable a concentration to be made at any selected point for an advance across the rivers into East Prussia in the direction of Königsberg. Here a double attack on converging lines is possible if Russia could assemble her forces rapidly enough and in sufficient numbers to invade East Prussia both from the Niemen and from the Polish triangle.

Before estimating the resources of Russia for attack, a word must be said about the influence of the naval situation on the land campaign. It is obvious that if Russia had full command of the Baltic Sea it would be possible to combine coast attacks with the land operations, and this would be a serious matter for the German generals charged with defence of the long belt of territory between the Russian border and the shores of the Baltic.

But in the opening stages of the Great War the command of the sea in this eastern theatre of operations was in the hands of Germany. This much gain she reaped from the creation of her battle-fleet. The Russian Navy—almost completely destroyed in the war with Japan—had been very dilatory in the work of reconstruction. At the outbreak of the war there was no Russian fleet in the waters of the Baltic that could venture to challenge the sea-power of Germany.

German naval supremacy in the Baltic

The British fleets were fully occupied in guarding the North Sea; and it would have been playing into the enemy's hands to detach any large force on such a mission as the passage of the narrow "Belts" that give access to the landlocked sea, passing through mine-strewn straits to meet the force that the Kiel Canal would enable Germany to concentrate more rapidly in the Baltic. The main Fleet of Britain could not be withdrawn from the North Sea, but Germany could have sent every one of her heaviest ships through the canal. It was therefore a necessity to leave her for a while the control of the Baltic. The Russian ships lay under the batteries of Cronstadt, their best use being to cover the approach to Petrograd and make it a dangerous matter for Germany to carry out a raid on Finland.

Воззваніе Верховнаго главнокомандующаго.

ПОЛЯКИ!

Пробилъ часъ, когда завѣтная мечта вашихъ отцовъ и дѣдовъ можетъ осуществиться.

Полтора вѣка тому назадъ живое тѣло Польши было растерзано на куски, но не умерла душа ея. Она жила надеждой, что наступитъ часъ воскресенія Польскаго народа, братскаго примиренія его съ Великой Россіей.

Русскія войска несутъ вамъ благую вѣсть этого примиренія.

Пусть сотрутся границы, разрѣзавшія на части Польскій народъ. Да возсоединится онъ во-едино подъ скипетромъ Русскаго Царя.

Подъ скипетромъ этимъ возродится Польша, свободная въ своей вѣрѣ, въ языкѣ, въ самоуправленіи.

Одного ждетъ отъ васъ Россія, — такого же уваженія къ правамъ тѣхъ народностей, съ которыми связала васъ исторія.

Съ открытымъ сердцемъ, съ братски протянутой рукой идетъ вамъ навстрѣчу Великая Россія. Она вѣритъ, что не заржавѣлъ мечъ, разившій врага при Гринвальдѣ.

Отъ береговъ Тихаго океана до Сѣверныхъ морей движутся Русскія рати.

Заря новой жизни занимается для васъ.

Да возсіяетъ въ этой зарѣ знаменіе Креста, — символъ страданія и воскресенія народовъ.

Верховный главнокомандующій
генералъ-адъютантъ НИКОЛАЙ.

THE DREAM OF POLAND TO BE REALISED.
The above picture is a reduced facsimile of the appeal issued to the Poles on August 16th, 1914, by the Grand Duke Nicholas, commander-in-chief of the Russian forces. The translation is on the right.

With the Germans thus in temporary command of the sea, it was necessary to keep a considerable force in Finland and about the northern capital. The German Fleet thus helped indirectly in the defence of the eastern frontier by diminishing the numbers immediately available for the attack upon it—one more instance of the far-reaching influence of sea-power.

Proclamation by the Commander-in-Chief.

POLES !

"The hour has sounded when the sacred dream of your fathers and your grandfathers may be realised. A century and a half has passed since the living body of Poland was torn in pieces, but the soul of the country is not dead. It continues to live, inspired by the hope that there will come for the Polish people an hour of resurrection and of fraternal reconciliation with Great Russia. The Russian Army brings you the solemn news of this reconciliation, which obliterates the frontiers, dividing the Polish peoples, which it unites conjointly under the sceptre of the Russian Tsar. Under this sceptre Poland will be born again, free in her religion and her language. Russian autonomy only expects from you the same respect for the rights of those nationalities to which history has bound you.

"With open heart and brotherly hand Great Russia advances to meet you. She believes that the sword, with which she struck down her enemies at Gruenwald, is not yet rusted. From the shores of the Pacific to the North Sea the Russian armies are marching. The dawn of a new life is beginning for you, and in this glorious dawn is seen the sign of the Cross, the symbol of suffering and of the resurrection of peoples."

The task of the Russian armies was not merely to defend the western border of the Empire, not merely to attack the frontiers of Germany and Austria-Hungary, but to deliver this attack in such force and at such an early date as to defeat the German plan of first crushing France and then transferring a portion of the German armies to the eastern theatre of war. Russia aimed at exerting such serious and early pressure as would force the German Empire to divert a part of the force employed against France to the east in the first weeks of the campaign, thus indirectly helping to decide the conflict in Western Europe.

Reason for Russia's swift action

What was the force that the Tsar's generals might hope to place in line on the Niemen, the Narev, and the Vistula? The military power of Russia, so far as mere numbers are a measure of such power, is the most formidable

SQUADRON OF RUSSIAN COSSACKS, EACH MAN OF WHICH PROVIDES HIS OWN HORSE.

CELEBRATING THE RUSSIAN VICTORIES IN GALICIA BEFORE THE WINTER PALACE, PETROGRAD.

RUSSIAN CAVALRY ON THE MARCH—THE POWER OF ENDURANCE OF BOTH MEN AND HORSES IS PROVERBIAL.

in Europe. But there has been not a little exaggeration about these numbers. Wild rumours circulated in the first days of the war that the Russians were mobilising " eight millions " of men. No serious authority on the subject has ever placed the armed forces of the Tsar's Empire at this enormous total.

Russian military strength

Russia maintains three armies—the army in Europe, the army of Siberia and the Far East, and the army of the Caucasus and Central Asia. Her armies are recruited under a law of universal liability to military service, but this does not mean that every man serves in the Army or receives the training of a soldier. The numbers available each year are far beyond the limits of the existing organisation. The men that are wanted are taken by a principle of selection among those who have reached their twentieth year. The recruit then serves for three years in the infantry or artillery, and for four if he is allotted to the cavalry or engineers. He is then passed into the reserve, to which he belongs for fourteen or fifteen years, so as to make up a total service in the first line of eighteen years.

The soldier is about thirty-eight years of age when he has completed his active and reserve service. He is then borne for another five years on the rolls of the Militia or Territorial Army (the Opolchenie, to give it its Russian name). At forty-three he is at last free from any further obligation of military service. The Cossacks of the south serve under another system. A Cossack is liable to be called out for service as long as he has health and strength to bear arms.

If the whole of the annual contingent of men liable for service were enrolled in the Army there would be over 600,000 recruits to be armed, equipped, and trained each year, and with a three to four years' service there would be considerably over two million men permanently with the colours. No State could bear such a burden. As a matter of fact, the peace footing of all the armies of Russia united before the war reached about 1,700,000 men, which was an unusually large figure, and due to the retention of time-expired men with the colours. It is the European Army of Russia, with its reserves, that counts in the first weeks of a Polish campaign, owing to the remoteness of the armies in the Caucasus, Central Asia, and Siberia.

THE HEEL OF WAR IN BALTIC RUSSIA.
When the Germans raided the Aland Islands and bombarded Libau and Bona, the Russians destroyed the port and station of Hango, on the north shore of the Gulf of Finland, to prevent it falling into their hands. The station is seen burning in the upper picture, and in the lower is a photograph of the ruined port. These were among the earliest of camera records of actual war conditions in Russia.

The first line of this Army is made up of twenty-seven army corps, a number of rifle brigades, and twenty cavalry divisions. Two of the army corps are formed of picked men with an extra standard of height, the " Guards Corps " at Petrograd, and the " Grenadier Corps " at Moscow. The other twenty-five army corps are each recruited from a province or group of provinces; but as the bulk of the Army has its peace stations west of Moscow, many of these corps are not actually posted in their recruiting districts. The Guards and Grenadier Corps have each three infantry divisions; the line corps have two each in peace and three in war. The war strength of a line corps is about 45,000 men, or, if a cavalry division is attached to it, about 50,000.

The regular cavalry is organised in twenty divisions (two of the Guard, fifteen of the line, two mixed divisions of Cossacks and line cavalry, and a Cossack division). This makes a force of about 80,000 sabres. Besides this there is the general levy of Cossack cavalry. The Cossack is bound to service through all his active life; he is partly trained at home, partly at a military centre. But he is no longer the ragged, irregular spearman of the Napoleonic wars. He is a disciplined soldier, usually serving as a cavalryman. There are also Cossack batteries of artillery and Cossack rifle battalions.

THE TRAIL OF THE HUN ALONG THE RUSSIAN FRONTIER WAS THE SAME AS IN BELGIUM.

This special drawing, based upon authentic notes from Russia, depicts some stalwart soldiers of the Tsar standing aghast as they come upon a scene just left by retreating Germans, who had pursued the policy of terrorism taught them by their war lords from the Kaiser down—a policy that made the villages of industrious Belgium a monument of eternal shame that centuries of repentance, oceans of tears, and a hundred war indemnities could not hope to remove.

WHERE THREE EMPIRES MEET—AN HISTORIC CORNER OF EUROPE.

This is the meeting point of three great Empires—the Russian, the German, and the Austrian—and is known as "Three Emperors' Corner." The hither side of the River Przemsza is in Silesia, in Germany; on the far side is Galicia, in Austria; and Russia is in the background, beyond the tributary stream. The spot is north-east of Cracow.

Besides the troops of the first line, there are with the colours two other classes. First there are the "reserve troops." This is a somewhat misleading name, unless their purpose is explained, for they are not reservists. They are really the skeleton cadres (organisations of officers with a small contingent of men), kept up to form a basis for the mobilisation of some of the large numbers of men who, on a general mobilisation, are not required to bring the first-line troops up to war strength. In the same way, the "fortress troops" permanently stationed in the inland fortified places and at the coast defences are skeleton units that are brought up to full strength on a mobilisation.

It is quite true that, considering the long period of service in the reserve, an enormous number of reservists are not only available on paper, but really exist. It must be remembered, however, that even though the men for the rank and file are available, and have had some training in past years, an army of many millions cannot be created by a mere decree. All that can be done at the outset is to fill up the existing units with the colours and the skeleton cadres, and to supply the men called out with arms, equipment, and stores from the mobilisation depots. After this stage the possession of large reserves of men serves to fill up the gaps made by loss in battle, and by the wear and tear of the campaign, and at the same time enables new units to be gradually created.

Russian plan of mobilisation

The Russian plan of mobilisation includes (1) bringing the first-line army up to war strength; (2) embodying sufficient of the surplus reservists to form, on the basis of the existing reserve cadres, a number of reserve battalions, squadrons, and batteries; (3) bringing the skeleton units of the fortress troops up to full strength in the same way, from the older classes of reservists; (4) calling up a considerable force of Cossack cavalry; and (5) calling out the Territorials, or Militia, for local defence and the preservation of order, and to supply troops to hold the lines of communication of the field army.

A mobilisation on these lines would give about three million men, with some 6,000 guns, for the first-line army, though the whole of this force would not be available at once; for even though the peace stations are arranged to facilitate concentration, want of a fully organised railway system makes it necessary to give time for reservists to travel long distances to join their units, and concentration has to be made by a small number of main lines.

With the Publishers' Cases Only

Artistic title-page and index to volume, splendid frontispiece consisting of a fine photogravure of Admiral Jellicoe

Not only are the publishers' cases the best value obtainable, but readers who secure them will have the satisfaction of knowing that with them ***and with them only*** will be given an artistic title-page and index to the volume, and a splendid frontispiece for the volume, consisting of a magnificent photogravure portrait of Admiral Jellicoe.

THE GREAT WAR as a book, therefore, is not complete without the publishers' registered cases, for in no other way can one obtain these additions so necessary to the completeness of a beautiful book.

For those whose choice must be Cloth or nothing, the publishers are issuing, at the very low price of 2/6, the exceedingly serviceable case illustrated below, which is as good as cloth binding can be.

This case is made of the best English cloth, described by binders as "full cloth extra." It is of a rich wine colour, and bears a handsome design blocked in black on the side, while the title on the back is in gold. The boards are extra thick, with bevelled edges.

As has already been stated, Half Leather binding is the best value and should be secured by all who can possibly afford it, but it is better to get even the Cloth than to let the parts lie about and become tattered and torn.

Whichever binding you choose, do it now!

THE PUBLISHERS' CLOTH BINDING

[*Photo: Topical*

A.S.C. REPAIR SHOP AT THE FRONT

THE ARMY SERVICE CORPS is the highly important body which looks after the welfare of the fighting "Tommy" in the firing-line. Above photograph (taken on a French road) shows a Portable Repair Shop attached to the British Motor Transport. The picture is an instance of the multifarious duties that are needed to supply for the welfare of an Army in being, and emphasises the yeoman part played by Petrol in the present stupendous campaign.

PRATT'S

Motor Spirit

is used by the British War Office and Admiralty for haulage of big field pieces, for heavy ammunition and food transport per motor-lorry, for reconnoitring per armoured motor-car, for aeroplane and seaplane reconnaissances, for despatch riding per motor-cycle, and for Red Cross Ambulances conveying wounded from the seat of action to the Hospitals at the base.

N.B.—Pratt's enjoys the full confidence of the Allies, who are using it in enormous quantities.

By Appointment.

Anglo-American Oil Co., Ltd.,  *36, Queen Anne's Gate, London, S.W*

0 Printed and published by the AMALGAMATED PRESS, LIMITED, The Fleetway House, Farringdon Street, London, E.C.
Published by Gordon & Gotch in Australia and New Zealand; by The Central News Agency, Ltd., in South Africa; by The Standard Literature Co., 13/1, Old Court House Street, Calcutta; and The Imperial News Co., Toronto and Montreal in Canada. *Advertisement applications should be made to The Advertisement Manager, The Fleetway House, Farringdon Street, London, E.C.*

Week ending November 7th, 1914.] [Registered for Canadian Magazine Post.

Part 12. **The Wonders of Aircraft in the War Copiously Illustrated.** **6d. Net.**

General Pau, one of France's most famous Commanders.

AN ENDURING BINDING FOR AN ENDURING WORK

As THE GREAT WAR begins to grow into a book, the question of binding in enduring form this permanent record of the mighty conflict will occupy the minds of readers.

The publishers are in the position to offer the best possible value in beautiful and durable bindings.

Before the advance in the cost of leather caused by the war, they had the foresight to make an advantageous contract for large supplies at the old price. Readers who buy the publishers' cases will, therefore, get the benefit of this contract, and may congratulate themselves in securing remarkably fine cases at a remarkably low figure. Every 16 parts will constitute a volume, but readers are urged to give an order at once to their newsagent or bookseller for the binding they require. The binding illustrated below is the Half Leather, which combines durability and elegance in a remarkable degree, and is well worth a great deal more than the difference in cost between it and the Cloth. This binding has a full gilt back, while the leather has been dyed a rich scarlet. The sides are reinforced at the corners with specially thick leather covering.

Bound in the publishers' Half Leather cases, the volumes of THE GREAT WAR will enhance the finest library.

The price is but 4/6.

(Turn to page III. of cover.)

PUBLISHERS' HALF-LEATHER BINDING

Probably in the first month of the war about a million and a half men would be pushed up to the actual front. One can only make rough estimates in such a case. But another million would rapidly become available. All the first line could not be sent to the front. It would be impossible entirely to strip Finland and the Petrograd and Moscow districts of all regular troops, and the garrisons of Poland would absorb some of the first-line men until the situation became quite clear.

In two ways the second-line troops would be of immediate help to the Army after a first success had made it possible to push forward into hostile territory. The fortress troops, whose numbers on mobilisation would rise to about a quarter of a million, would supply the siege train to Russian armies in the field, and could also mobilise a number of heavy batteries. The mobilisation tables include the formation of four hundred and fifty battalions of infantry and seventy-two squadrons of cavalry out of the Territorial Army—some 500,000 men. These could be moved up to guard the lines of communication, and the fortress troops would help, if necessary, by sending garrison detachments to hold captured fortresses of the enemy.

The field army would thus be kept up to its full fighting strength, by (1) receiving a constant stream of reservists, and (2) not having to leave any detachments in its rear as it pushed forward. In this way the second-line troops and the great mass of reservists available make the Russian Army a particularly formidable fighting force. We may estimate the field armies at two millions of men in the front line, with at least 500,000 more to support them and take charge of all the services in rear of the fighting-front.

In a long war the numbers of the active Army could be very considerably increased. It is estimated that, after completing the mobilisation, some two million reservists and territorials would still be available for further levies, all of them men who have had some Army service. Besides these, there would be at least seven million men of military age who had never been in the ranks. These large numbers are what lead some writers to tell of armies of six or eight million men mustering at the call of the White Tsar. But it must be remembered that it would be extremely difficult to find cadres of efficient leaders, officers and non-commissioned officers, for such enormous levies, and almost impossible to furnish them with the necessary proportion of batteries, manned by trained gunners. Even for the three or four millions that Russia should gradually be able to accumulate at the fighting-front, the difficulty of providing competent officers and sergeants for anything beyond the first-line units is a serious one—all the more serious because Russia is a country in which education is in a very backward state. In many of the provinces fifty per cent. of the adult population cannot read or write.

The enormous Russian reserves

But, apart from this, there would be no real gain in putting

GERMAN DESTROYERS LEAVING KIEL HARBOUR WITH A ZEPPELIN OVERHEAD.
The largest Zeppelins at the opening of the war were known to be capable of a speed of fifty-two miles an hour without any favouring wind, and to possess a radius of over twelve hundred miles, so that they could have made a return trip from Kiel or Heligoland over the North Sea, Great Britain, and the Irish Sea, to Dublin or Belfast.

MM

EXAMPLES OF THE TORPEDO-SHAPED GERMAN MONOPLANES.

This is a representative type of flying machine used by the German Army. The form of the body and the curve of the wings mark it out as different from the more common Etrich-taube type of machine, which was much favoured by German airmen. The pilot is controlling the engine, which is just about to start, and the observer is seen sitting behind.

armies of many millions into the field. Mere numbers do not give victory in war, for effective force and numbers are not the same thing. If half-trained multitudes are pushed to the front, the difficulty of supply increases to breakdown point; and even if all needs of the men could be supplied, there is no front on which such vast armies could be brought into action. The presence of idle myriads behind the fighting-front is an encumbrance, not a gain, and the mere crowding of men up to the battle-line may be their destruction. There comes a moment when Attila's grim words are true once more: "The thicker the grass, the easier we shall mow it down."

The Russian soldier is a good fighting-man. He is obedient, enduringly patient under trial, stolidly reckless of wounds and death, easily inspired with the idea that the war is something of a crusade, and thus animated by a touch, not of fanatic ardour, but of a quiet zeal for the work that will carry him through toil, danger, and hardship with an even mind. Long tradition, summed up in Suvaroff's famous saying, "The bullet is a fool—the bayonet counts," gives him a healthy longing to close with cold steel. A million and a half of such men are splendid material for a fighting force.

But then comes the question of leadership. It must be confessed that in recent wars the record of Russian generalship and Russian Army administration was disappointing. In the war with Turkey the Russian army narrowly escaped destruction. In the war with Japan it had an unbroken

GERMAN AIRSHIP OF THE "PARSEVAL" TYPE.

This is an airship of the non-rigid type, and in this respect, as well as in many others it differs materially from the Zeppelin. At the opening of war Germany and her ally were the only countries possessing Zeppelins, but Britain, France, Russia, and Japan possessed airships of the type shown above.

TYPES OF GERMAN AEROPLANES WIDELY USED IN THE WAR.
It will be observed that seven of these flying-machines are monoplanes. They are of the famous "Taube" type—or, to give them their full title, "Etrich-Taube." Etrich was the name of their inventor, and "Taube" is the German word for dove. The unique feature of these machines is that they are constructed throughout of steel, giving them great rigidity. Of the three biplanes, or "doppel-deckers"—two on the extreme left and one second from the left at the back—one is of the "arrow" type.

record of failure, redeemed by the heroism of the men. Much has been done since the close of the war with Japan to improve the administration of the Army and raise the level of military education among the officers, but eight years is not a long time in which to effect any serious change in such a huge organisation. But there are, and always have been, brilliant soldiers in the upper grades of the Russian Army.

A LEVIATHAN AND A MOSQUITO OF THE AIR.
These two types of aircraft represent the two wings of the service—the Zeppelin that can carry a ton and a half of high explosives to be dropped upon the point attacked, and the aeroplane, whose value lies chiefly in reconnaissance work, in inspecting the enemy's positions, and in guiding the artillery in attack.

At the beginning of the Great War Russia possessed three leaders of high reputation—Rennenkampf, a cavalry general, and the commander of one of the subsidiary armies under Kuropatkin in the Japanese War; Samsonoff, who had also fought in the Far East, and had the reputation of a first-class military organiser; and Russky, a scientific soldier, with a good record as a teacher of the art of war in the Russian Staff College.

All three were among the commanders sent to the western frontier. Russia had the good fortune to be opposed to German and Austrian armies that could not take the field in full strength. Germany had to send most of her first-line troops across the Rhine, and could concentrate on the eastern frontier of her empire at most five regular army corps (say, from 200,000 to 250,000 men), reinforced with reserve and Landwehr units. Austria had to leave a large army to operate against Servia, to guard her southern frontier against possible dangers from Italy, and to keep the peace in her Slav provinces.

The Slav and Czech regiments sent to the front in Galicia were doubtful elements of strength. They might even prove a danger and a weakness. Russia could therefore count upon having to deal with opponents so heavily handicapped at the outset that she might hope to force them to act upon the defensive at an early stage of the campaign, and thus obtain the precious advantage of the initiative for herself.

She had a further and unexpected gain. It was generally said, even amongst her Allies, that the Russian armies could not concentrate any considerable force at the front before the middle of September. But, thanks partly to many of the units having been brought up to high peace-strength before the crisis; thanks, further, to enormous exertions made by the Staff and the railway administration, by the middle of August the army in Poland itself had been heavily reinforced and was ready for active operations, and other great masses of mobilised troops had assembled on the right along the line of the Narev and the Niemen, and south of the Pripet region, on the left, threatening the frontiers of Eastern Galicia.

Russian swiftness of mobilisation

GERMAN "AGO" MILITARY BIPLANE.

Without anticipating the story of the campaign we may here note how the pieces were set for the dread game of war on this eastern borderland of Russia. So far as one can see through the proverbial "fog of war," no fewer than six armies were set in motion by the Tsar's generals. On the right two columns advanced from the Niemen and Narev, the first in the direction of Königsberg, south of the Pregel, through the Masurian lake-land, the march being rendered easier by the exceptionally dry season of the summer of 1914; the second moved on its left through the forest tract west of the Narev line.

ZEPPELIN ENTERING ITS FLOATING SHED AT FRIEDRICHSHAFEN.

The Lake of Constance, or the Boden See, as the Germans call it, is partly in German territory and partly in Switzerland. It has many floating sheds for airships along the German side, and the photograph shows one near the German town of Friedrichshafen.

In the centre, based on the Polish triangle, an army was pushed forward towards the frontiers of the provinces of Posen and Silesia, and to cover the flank of this advance another army was sent up the Vistula, to check the menace of an Austrian army in this direction.

GERMAN BIPLANE STARTING ON SCOUTING EXPEDITION.

This Austrian march on the Vistula was itself threatened in flank by an advance of the fifth Russian army into Eastern Galicia, and a sixth Russian army into the Bukovina.

It will be seen at once that this vast game of war was a very complicated one. It was quite possible for any of the armies operating on the frontiers of Russian Poland to have its position endangered by a check, not to its own advance, but to that of its nearest comrades. The strongly fortified central position of the Polish triangle provided, however, a kind of pivot for the operations of the centre.

THE FORMIDABLE GERMAN MONSTER OF THE THIRD ELEMENT.

The drawing on the left illustrates a set of ideal conditions for an attack by airship. A stratum of heavy cloud hangs rather low, and makes the land below experience "a dull day," while the airship, floating in the sunlight above the cloud, progresses with ease, its huge bulk hidden from the earth. From the cage suspended through the cloud, and visible only with extreme difficulty, the navigators above can be instructed as to the route, and bombs can be dropped upon selected spots. The drawing on the right shows how hard it is to detect an airship on a moonless night. It is only by a powerful searchlight that it can be seen, and it will be noticed that the part not in the direct rays of the searchlight beams is invisible. The value of powerful searchlights for purposes of defence will be apparent.

"FIRE ON THESE MACHINES."
This is a reproduction of a printed notice issued by the military authorities to French soldiers, so that they might be able to recognise hostile German aircraft.

Success at the outset of a campaign has an influence of the highest value upon the armies engaged. In this case the Russians had the prospect of securing fairly easy victories at the outset, and, at the very least, the certainty of being able to march far into hostile territory without having any very serious obstacle to overcome. It was not likely that the German armies, weakened as they were by the very conditions under which the war opened, would attempt any stubborn resistance in advance of the line of fortresses along the lower Vistula and at the extremities of the Frisches Haff. And it was quite certain that the Austrians would not make any prolonged resistance in Eastern Galicia. Their first serious stand would not be met until the neighbourhood of Przemysl was reached.

Austria had hoped that at the outset of the war she could add to her own forces and increase the difficulties of the Russian commanders by exciting a rising in Poland. The Galician army corps, made up of Polish soldiers, would be the vanguard of her advance along the Vistula, and arms and ammunition for the expected insurrection had been collected on the border. The Polish associations of Galicia and Posen had issued a proclamation to their "brethren of Russian Poland."

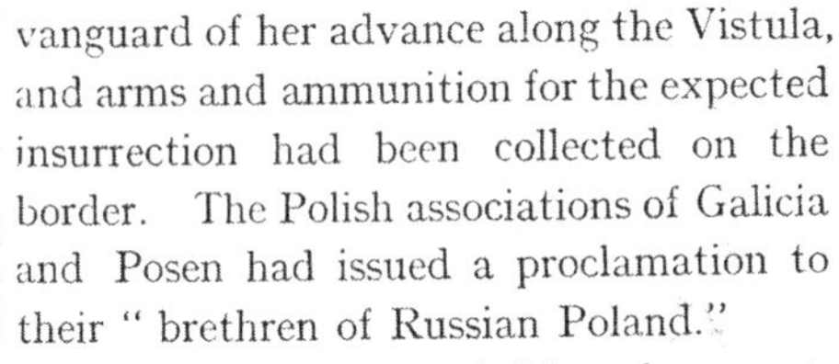

It was a remarkable document. Instead of warlike eloquence, there was a warning not to attempt a rising, not even to collect arms, till the Austrian vanguard had arrived and secured a first victory. Then all the arms they wanted would be given to them.

Meanwhile, they were told to make up their minds to act, and to provide themselves, not with military equipment, but with good, sound boots, "two pairs of socks, two shirts, a rough working suit, a cap, and a bag to hang by a strap over the shoulder." It was the most matter-of-fact document ever drafted by an insurrectionary committee.

But the Tsar had issued a proclamation making larger promises than any committee could put forward. To Poland he promised Home Rule when the victory over Germany and Austria was won, and with this self-government and liberty of laws, religion, and language he promised the reconstitution of the old Polish territory, by the annexation of Posen and Galicia. Poland was to live again as an autonomous State under the Russian Crown. There is no doubt that the proclamation had a great effect on Polish national opinion. It paralysed any plans of insurrection by dividing the leaders of the Poles. Many of them saw in a Russian success the prelude to a restoration of their national life. Thus the great conflict began with a pledge that, if the Russian armies were victorious, their victory would be followed by the resurrection of the Polish nation, inauguarating a new era of peace and goodwill in Europe.

THE ENORMOUS SIZE OF A ZEPPELIN.
If we stand on the roadway of Ludgate Hill, London, and look up at the dome of St. Paul's Cathedral, and if we are told that a Zeppelin is about fifty per cent. longer than the distance from the ground to the top of the golden cross, we begin to realise how enormous is one of these great airships.

AIRCRAFT OF THE ROYAL FLYING CORPS.

CHAPTER XVII.

THE NEW ARM IN THE NEW ELEMENT.

By an Expert in Aviation.

Former Use of Aircraft in War—Purpose of the New Arm in Warfare—Types of Airships—Frameless and Semi-rigid Types—The Zeppelin—Construction, Speed, and Capacity of Zeppelins—Aeroplanes—Aeroplane Powers of Attack on Dirigibles—Variable Speed—The Fuel Question—The Training of Airmen—German Secret Preparation—Aircraft in Naval Warfare—The Air Equipment of the Different Belligerents—The Question of Motors—The British Royal Flying Corps—Tributes to Its Value and Efficiency—Aircraft as Range-finders—Air Raids

THE most novel feature of the greatest war in history was the fact that it was waged in three elements, and not confined to two—land and water—as former wars True, in the Italian campaign in Tripoli, airships and aeroplanes were used not infrequently to locate the enemy. But that was not war in the air, in that the enemy possessed no means of ascending from the ground and matching the equipment and advantages enjoyed by the Italians.

In the Balkan Wars, too, some slight use was made of aeroplanes for purposes of reconnaissance. Here again the numbers possessed were very few, and the flying was of a character that would not be called military in any sense of the word by the Great Powers who engaged in the world's greatest conflict. France and Germany have been the pioneers of aerial warfare, with Britain as a very good third. All the great States fighting on the Continent of Europe started the war equipped with highly-developed aircraft—airships or dirigibles, aeroplanes, and seaplanes (or aeroplanes with floats for use at sea)—and all had carefully-trained pilots and aerial observers.

A GROUP OF BELGIAN MILITARY AVIATORS.
The photograph was taken in Ghent, which this party of Belgian flying-men had reached from Namur before the latter city had fallen under heavy battering by the big German siege-guns.

Thus for the first time we were engaged in war in the air, because the opposing forces had the men and the machines. As it is a prime object of developing such a Third Arm to reap an advantage over the opponent by its possession, it follows that it was impossible any longer to confine aerial work in connection with warfare to the business of spying on the foe. That foe was also in the air to prevent his antagonist observing him. It was as vital that his enemy should fail in achieving that purpose as it was that he should succeed in spying on the enemy. That, in brief, is the why and wherefore of airman attacking airman; of the dirigible balloon stealing over forts, undefended areas, and camps to drop bombs on them

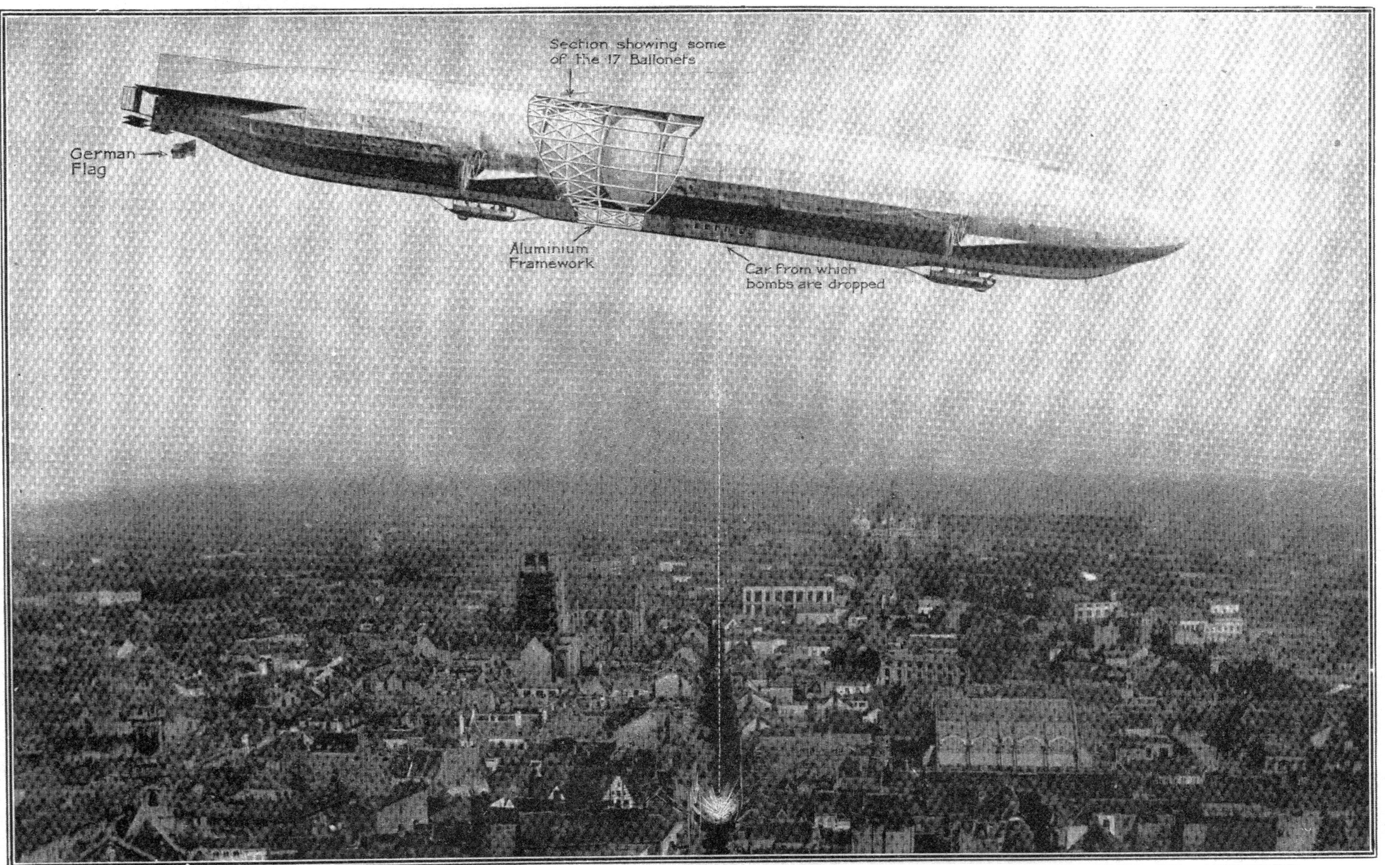

DIAGRAMMATIC REPRESENTATION OF A ZEPPELIN DROPPING A BOMB ON THE ILL-FATED CITY OF ANTWERP.

One of these great scourges of the sky caused havoc in Antwerp before the fall of the city on October 9th, 1914, although children, women, and old men were the chief sufferers. The cut-away section of the side of the airship illustrates the construction of these monsters of the upper air. The rigid grey-coloured body contains **seventeen separate balloons, each of which can be filled independently** of all the others, and injury to one section does not affect the other balloons. A Zeppelin carries two cars with a long passage, really part of the main framework, between the two, as seen in the picture. Many of the Zeppelins are fitted with a platform right on top of the body, and this platform is mounted with a special sky-pointing gun, so as to fire upon aeroplane attack from above.

in the dead of night; and of aeroplanes and seaplanes flying by day, some with small bombs that can be released when over the objective, others with machine-guns; yet others with sharpshooters. The tale of all these doings stirs the blood, and suggests unlimited scope for patriotic adventure.

France has always made a feature of the frameless airship, in which the gasbag is merely an envelope of fabric, without anything rigid in it. The great military value of this system is that such a machine is easy to transport from point to point by rail or motor-car in a collapsed condition. It can be inflated at a convenient place with compressed hydrogen available in cylinders. Such an airship in the field need not be operated from a gigantic and easily-detectable airship hall, because of this power of collapsing it and inflating it at will. Usually, however, to save cost and time, when the conditions of the campaign render it safe, portable sheds are employed for housing the larger sorts of French dirigibles.

The smaller airships, such as are used by Britain, can be moored in the open. Some of the large vessels of the semi-rigid sort can also be moored in the open even in high winds, if the car, or gondola, containing the power plant is temporarily detached. The envelopes of both these types of dirigibles are made of gas-tight, rubber-proofed fabric, which deteriorates rapidly, especially under the action of daylight. Where gas-leaks occur however, the envelopes can be patched to quite a remarkable extent; hence they are good for several seasons, even when exposed.

For making voyages of some distance, especially for offensive work, when heavy bombs have to be carried as well as large supplies of fuel, large airships are essential. The biggest French vessels were only a fraction more than half the size of the monster, rigid German airships of over four hundred and fifty feet in length. Even so, however, some of the French airships were over three hundred and thirty-six feet long.

The outstanding characteristics of the French school of design are the frameless and the semi-rigid systems, which can readily be emptied or collapsed, just as the rigid dirigible is the outstanding, but by no

THE BULLET-PROOF CAGE OF THE ZEPPELIN BOMB-THROWER.
When the Zeppelin floats in safety, hidden above the clouds, it can drop through the misty screen an armoured cage, like that shown here, from which observations can be made and bombs discharged in comparative safety, as it is extremely difficult to distinguish so small an object from the earth.

NN

A ZEPPELIN CREW WATCHING ANOTHER AERIAL BATTLESHIP.

Experience showed that the occupation of a Zeppelin airman is the most dangerous it is possible to conceive. Accident or the vagaries of the weather have sent two Zeppelins to earth and their entire crews to death. This photograph shows the crew of a Zeppelin watching the operations of another Zeppelin that is sailing past.

means the only, type of airship produced by Germany. Count Zeppelin, that splendid German veteran, whose daring cavalry reconnaissances won him fame in the early stages of the Franco-German War of 1870-1, acquired the patents of an Austrian engineer named Schwarz, who had constructed the hull of a dirigible in Russia, and another in Germany, both of the thinnest aluminium sheeting, but rendered rigid by cross-bracing, girder fashion, with aluminium tubing. With this development, Count von Zeppelin resuscitated an original idea by connecting to a rigid framework several balloons placed one behind the other. He discarded Schwarz's rigid aluminium outer hull. A Zeppelin airship consists of a lattice-work cylinder having from sixteen to twenty-four sides in cross section, and built of aluminium tube girders, rigidly braced internally. The vessels have varied in size, for those built in 1908 were only half the size of the largest produced before the opening of war. They also differed one from another in the precise section, and in the number of interior balloons. But from start to finish there was no departure from the main principles of construction.

The cylindrical aluminium frame which gives the vessel its distinctive shape is divided longitudinally into sixteen or more compartments, each with

A GERMAN HIGH-ANGLE GUN FOR ATTACKING AIRCRAFT.

The creation of the air arm of warfare immediately called into being a class of anti-aircraft guns specially designed for counter-attack. These take many forms, and some are wonderful pieces of scientific mechanism. This photograph shows a German aircraft-attacking gun caisson mounted on a motor-tractor so as to give the maximum of mobility. The special recoil-resistance apparatus is seen at the side of the wheel. Even the enemies of Germany cannot refuse their meed of admiration for the veteran Count Zeppelin (seen above) who, by indomitable perseverance in face of disaster, brought the Zeppelin airship to a high point of practical efficiency.

DISEMBARKING A BRITISH AEROPLANE ON ITS ARRIVAL IN FRANCE.

Here is seen one of our Army aeroplanes—minus its wings—being hoisted over the side of a British transport on arrival in France. As a matter of fact, however, few of the British air machines were shipped over—they were nearly all flown across, despite the fact that not one of them had floats of any kind to help it to remain on the surface if it had been necessary to descend while crossing the Channel. One British airman flew aeroplanes over from England to the front on eight consecutive days, returning every day by train, boat, and motor-car ready for another. He also did some aerial reconnaissance work at the front, and was slightly wounded.

self-complete balloon or hydrogen gasbag, fitted with a valve for emptying it of gas, and an appendage for inflating it with hydrogen, as well as an automatic safety-valve to limit the maximum pressure of gas inside. The largest Zeppelins have over 812,000 cubic feet gas capacity, and are more than 500 feet long, yet they have a maximum diameter of less than fifty feet, so that they present a minimum of head resistance to forward travel, particularly as the cars fore and aft, each with its two motors (of 180 to 200 horse-power apiece) and set of two propellers, are placed as close as can be against the big hull. Thus only the long sausage-form has to be pushed through the air, in contradistinction to the semi-rigid and frameless forms of construction, in which car and power plant are one unit, and the gasbag or balloon an independent one above them, and in which the driving effort is not applied to the main mass to be pushed through the air, but is delivered on a lower plane from the car.

DROPPING THE DEADLY AIR BOMB.
The task of dropping the bomb is the work of the observer, who sits behind the pilot, as seen here.

With a Zeppelin the thrust of the propellers is delivered from the sides of the main envelope, resulting in better mechanical efficiency. Aluminium is used for the construction of the cars. Each car has a double bottom, protected by strong rubber buffers, to render the vessel equally suitable for alighting on the surface of the water or on land. The propellers are fixed on stays to the side of the balloon, and are gear-driven from the engines contained in the cars, which also carry ammunition and guns. A unique Zeppelin feature is that the rigid frame of the gasbags enables a gun platform to be mounted on the top of the balloon, so that this was the only airship in the world the captain and crew of which could be warned by look-out men when anything is flying above and threatening the craft. However, experiments before the war showed that danger to the craft was caused by the detonation of a gun on top of it. But in war, risks have to be taken which in peace would not be faced until investigation and experiment had led to further development. The largest Zeppelins are capable of a speed, independent of the wind, of quite fifty-two miles an hour. They have a radius of action of at least twelve hundred miles. This means that, operating from Kiel or Heligoland, they could go to Dublin or Belfast and back. They possess the longest radius of action of any class of aircraft in the world, and they are much the speediest dirigible balloons. They can also carry loads of about five tons, but this must include the weight of the crew and of fuel, oil, and water, so that the weight of ammunition carried could not well exceed a ton and a half. They hold the world's

THE ZEPPELIN SHED AT DÜSSELDORF.
The enormous sheds, or " hangars," necessary for housing the Zeppelins make them conspicuous objects, so that they form easy marks for attack by daring flying men. Flight-Lieutenant C. H. Collet was the first to fly into German territory, where he dropped a bomb on the shed at Düsseldorf on September 23rd, 1914. The bomb set fire to the shed, but it was impossible to estimate what damage had been done.

Some Heroes of Our Royal Flying Corps

The central portrait is Commander Samson; on the extreme left is Flight-Commander R. L. G. Marix, who raided Dusseldorf; next is Mr. Walter Wood, who escaped after capture by Germans; on the extreme right Captain Robin Grey, who received the Legion of Honour; and on his right Squadron-Commander Gerrard.

Lieutenant S. V. Sippe, reported on Oct. 9th, 1914, to have taken part in an air raid that damaged the Zeppelin sheds at Dusseldorf.

Sir David Henderson, commanding the Royal Flying Corps, was warmly commended in the dispatch of October 8th, 1914.

Squadron-Commander Spenser D. A. Gray, R.N., carried out the air raid on the Dusseldorf Zeppelin hangar on October 9th, 1914.

Flight-Lieutenant C. H. Collet made the first attack on the German sheds at Dusseldorf, as announced officially on September 23rd, 1914.

Mr. Gordon Bell was shot, and had his machine smashed by Germans at Mons, but managed to plane to earth and rejoin the British lines.

Lieutenant A. Christie, attached to the Royal Field Artillery, mentioned in Sir John French's dispatch of October 8th, 1914.

A group of members of the Royal Flying Corps, including Lieutenant Playfair, Lieutenant Mills, Lieutenant Soames, Captain Board, Major Riley, Major Higgins, Lieutenant Jones, Lieutenant Gould, Lieutenant Small, and Lieutenant Andersen.

OFFICERS AND MEN OF THE ROYAL FLYING CORPS WITH THEIR MACHINES.

OFFICERS and men of the Royal Flying Corps wear a distinctive dress. The men wear a designation on their arm consisting of the words: "Royal Flying Corps," in white letters on a blue ground. Officers and men who have gained their flying certificate wear on their left breast a white badge consisting of two eagle wings.

The men wear a khaki-coloured undress uniform, with a coat that gives them, as it were, a breastplate of cloth across their chest. The military mechanicians, who are concerned with the maintenance of the engines, wear the ordinary blue overalls, their only distinguishing mark being the forage-cap, which can on occasion be pulled down to tie under the chin. One of these mechanicians is seen on the extreme left.

On the right is a sergeant of the R.F.C., wearing the new badge of a propeller on his arm. He is saluting two aviation officers, one dressed for flying, the other wearing the flying certificate badge. On the right is an army B.E. biplane, with its four-bladed propeller and two seats for pilot and observer. This type, it is stated, is becoming more and more the standard pattern of machine for use by the R.F.C. On the left is a Bleriot monoplane, and in the air a Henri Farman biplane.

HOW ZEPPELIN 5 WAS WRECKED AND CAPTURED BY RUSSIAN CAVALRY.

As a Russian cavalry brigade, with a horse battery, was proceeding towards the Russo-German frontier in September, 1914, Zeppelin 5 approached from the direction of Mlava. The battery promptly opened fire. At the third volley the airship began to assume a vertical inclination, its stabilisater and rudder being damaged. Flinging down ineffective bombs, the Zeppelin disappeared behind a wood. Without losing a moment, the guns were taken round the wood at a gallop and renewed their fire. The airship then slowly descended to earth and was captured, its crew of three officers and seven men being taken prisoners. One of the officers had torn off his epaulets to conceal his rank. The hull of the airship, which had been pierced in several places by the Russian fire, was eventually blown up, after several trophies had been carried off, including an Army flag with the name "Zeppelin 5" and an embroidered eagle insignia of merit.

record for dirigible balloon altitude at over 10,000 feet. The disadvantage of the system is that this form of construction can be used only from a permanent and specially-prepared base. Zeppelin airships not only want enormous accommodation by reason of their vast size, but they also need a regiment of men to handle them when they are starting and landing, and they require large crews. As many as thirty men have been found in a captured airship. In the event of storms arising they are practically unmanageable. They cannot be emptied of gas as can frameless and semi-rigid balloons. A mild breeze blowing on the side of a Zeppelin exercises a force of scores of tons, tossing and tumbling about a whole battalion of men engaged in endeavouring to restrain the monster.

Drawbacks of the Zeppelin

Because of this difficulty of controlling them in gales or bad weather, many Zeppelins were damaged or destroyed before the war began. Two of the greatest catastrophes in airship history befell the first two naval Zeppelins, L (or "luftschiff"—i.e., "airship") 1 and L2. L1 was engaged in manœuvres with the German High Sea Fleet on September 9th, 1913, when she was suddenly caught by a violent squall. The vessel was carried up five thousand feet, at which height the buoyancy of the gas-containers began to fail owing to an escape of gas. Rain fell in cataracts, and the cover held moisture to such an extent as to increase the weight to be sustained by one or two tons. At this juncture a fresh gust caught her and drove her downwards to the water, where she buckled, and sank, with the loss of fourteen of her crew.

Five weeks later, on October 17th, L2, a yet larger and more powerful Zeppelin, made an ascent from Johannisthal, near Berlin, with a crew of twenty-eight officers and men. As she rose the gas expanded and escaped

THE BRITISH ROYAL FLYING CORPS AT FARNBOROUGH.

The British Royal Flying Corps, under Sir David Henderson, did invaluable observation work, and soon established their worth as individually superior to the German aviator. In his despatch of September 7th, 1914, Sir John French wrote: "I wish particularly to bring to your lordship's notice the admirable work done by the Royal Flying Corps under Sir David Henderson. Their skill, energy, and perseverance have been beyond all praise. They have furnished me with the most complete and accurate information, which has been of incalculable value in the conduct of the operations. Fired at constantly both by friend and foe, and not hesitating to fly in every kind of weather, they have remained undaunted throughout. Further, by actually fighting in the air, they have succeeded in destroying five of the enemy's machines."

from the valves, which are located under the gasbags, and just above the cars. A spark from the magneto, or a back-fire from one of her four engines (each of 180 horse-power), probably set the gas on fire. A rush of flame was seen from the ground, there was a loud explosion or crash, and the blazing airship fell to the ground. All on board were killed.

Up to the date of these two accidents Count Zeppelin had been able to boast that no life has been lost in any of the mishaps to his airships. It says much for German resolution that the German Government proceeded, undismayed, to build additional ships of the same type. In Great Britain, unfortunately, a very minor mishap to naval airship No. 1, which was begun in 1910, led to the abandonment of rigid airship construction for the British Government until 1913, when Mr. Churchill gave orders for one large ship of this type to be commenced.

German faith in rigid airships

In the air all airships are controlled on practically the same principle, the differences being merely in the degree of navigability and in the portions of the airship to which the various control gears are fixed. The Zeppelin looks to the lay eye by far the most shipshape craft. The gasbag of an airship is nearly always furnished with something approximating to the fins of a fish, or else to the feathers on an arrow, so as to give it stability and prevent it from rolling. The most general method is to have horizontal and vertical fixed planes. There is, besides, a vertical rudder, or, in the case of a Zeppelin, a series of rudders, to enable the machine to turn to right or to left, so long as it is moving under its own power, and has steering way. Most airships carry water ballast for emergencies. By discharging it, the airship can be made to rise; but most dirigibles do not waste their supplies in this fashion. On the contrary, they rise or fall by the power of their engines. Some have screws that can exert power in a vertical direction to cause the machine to lift. This is not the general, or by any means the most efficient way. The ordinary method of rising is to employ horizontal rudders, otherwise movable aeroplane surfaces. Thus, for steering to right or left, the vertical rudder is turned to one side or the other. In like fashion, the horizontal rudders or planes are moved up or down, as the pilot wishes the airship to ascend or descend. The operation is, in effect, merely steering up or down, instead of to the right or left.

The naval and military departments of the leading countries of the world have realised that for effective work all classes of aircraft are required. This necessity primarily arose from the limited range of the aeroplane, which

TWO OF BRITAIN'S MILITARY AIRSHIPS.

The "Delta," nearest the camera, with the "Gamma" behind it, anchored at Gosport near their stations. The largest Zeppelins are more than three times as long as these British airships, and have an internal cubic capacity almost nine times as great.

A BRITISH SEAPLANE.

The need for aeroplanes that could alight on and rise from water was felt by Great Britain more than by any of the other belligerent countries, and this need led to the development of the seaplane as an arm of the British Navy.

is approximately half that of the Zeppelin dirigible balloon; from the proportionately low carrying capacity of aeroplanes; and, above all, from the fact that the aeroplane must continually travel, else it falls, whereas the dirigible balloon can hover or drift without using power and without losing altitude.

Of the two, the aeroplane is vastly the more weather-worthy, and as superior to the dirigible in speed as the airship is superior to it in range. No dirigible has yet developed a speed of a mile a minute, independent of the wind, though Count Zeppelin got very close to that rate of travel; whereas many aeroplanes have speeds of over two miles a minute, and have maintained that rate of travel for an hour at a spell. Until 1912, also, the use of the aeroplane was confined almost entirely to daylight, whereas, by contrast, for military operations, the use of the dirigible balloon has been and is confined largely to the hours of darkness. Only recently has it been possible to build dirigibles to rise to such heights as 10,000 feet. This contrasts with an altitude record of 26,000 feet for the aeroplane.

BRITISH MARINE AIRSHIP OF THE "ASTRA TORRES" TYPE OVER OSTEND.
This British airship is 250 feet long, which is almost twice as long as the two shown on the opposite page, and has a cubic capacity over four times as great, namely 8,700 cubic metres. Her speed is rather more than that of the best Zeppelin, being about fifty-two miles an hour.

Thus, with its greater speed, its presentation of proportionately an infinitesimal mark to fire when compared with the vast bulk of the dirigible balloon, its greater weather-worthiness, and its ability to ascend to more than double the height of the airship, as well as to turn, rise, and fall very much more quickly, the aeroplane has numerous advantages over the airship, which must necessarily be more or less at its mercy in daylight.

Further, thanks to the extraordinary enterprise of such pioneers as Commander C. R. Samson, head of the naval wing of the Royal Flying Corps, the aeroplane began to invade the peculiar province of the dirigible balloon by flying in the hours of darkness, an operation which necessarily calls for most exceptional nerve and skill. The aeroplane is therefore the most serious menace to the dirigible balloon when it is flying at over 6,000 feet, so as to be out of range of the gun fire from below. Moreover, both aeroplane and seaplane were equipped with bombs designed to burst either before or after actually making contact with the airship, so as to annihilate it by exploding the hydrogen in its gasbag. Early in this war we learned that piercing an airship's envelope with bullets is not an effectual method of compassing her destruction.

COMMANDER SAMSON, OF THE ROYAL NAVAL FLYING CORPS, AND SOME OF HIS OFFICERS.
The name of Commander Samson (seen seated fourth from the left) came prominently before the public in the early days of the war. On September 16th, 1914, in a small armoured motor-car he killed four Uhlans and captured a fifth, near Doullens, close to the Belgian frontier.

The naval and military requirements of the nations engaged in the war put a very high premium on a quality which the airship has always possessed, but which it was found possible to achieve with aeroplanes only during the twelvemonth prior to the war—widely variable speed in flight. Variable speed represents reserve energy, such as enables an aeroplane to rise quickly to a great height or to travel very fast. There are various reasons why we also want that same machine to be able to travel at considerably less than its maximum speed. The first aeroplane to fly at two miles a minute required a run over the best part of a mile before it would rise from the ground, and quite that space for a clear run on alighting—conditions obviously impossible for naval or military use. For those services aeroplanes are required which will rise after the briefest run, yet which will sustain themselves in the air at a slow rate of travel, so that the speed can be reduced to that rate in the act of alighting. Then there will be the least possible momentum to absorb before actually making contact with the ground or water and bringing the machine to a standstill.

Value of variable speed in aircraft

Aeroplanes will rise in fifty feet with a full load. They can be brought down into a field surrounded by trees, yet in flight they are required to develop high maximum of speeds of ninety or more miles an hour, and to be capable of flying at as low a speed as thirty-six miles an hour, or even less. Range of flying speed is, besides, necessary to ensure reliability, because no machinery will be dependable when worked to its limit without an instant's relief. Furthermore, to do a certain amount of flying at half or three-quarters speed effects an enormous saving of fuel, and therefore correspondingly increases the range of action of the machine.

It must be remembered that the flying machine has to carry its own fuel supplies into the air with it. In warfare its range of service is determined by the distance it can cover without replenishing supplies of any sort. With aircraft, as with warships, motor-cars, and all mechanical vehicles of travel, the rate of consumption of fuel increases out of all proportion to the increase of speed. Merely to double the horse-power developed is not to double the speed of the machine, but, owing to the increasing air resistance with higher speed, only to add a small percentage to the velocity.

Efficiency and fuel supply

It is astonishing how a comparatively few hours of flying begin to cause " warping " and loss of the original shape of the wing, with consequent loss of efficiency. In first-class high-speed machines a wing is rarely in perfect condition for more than one hundred and fifty or one hundred and sixty hours flying. After that time the wing begins to get out of shape, and the leading edge of the wings, instead of being straight and true, looks as

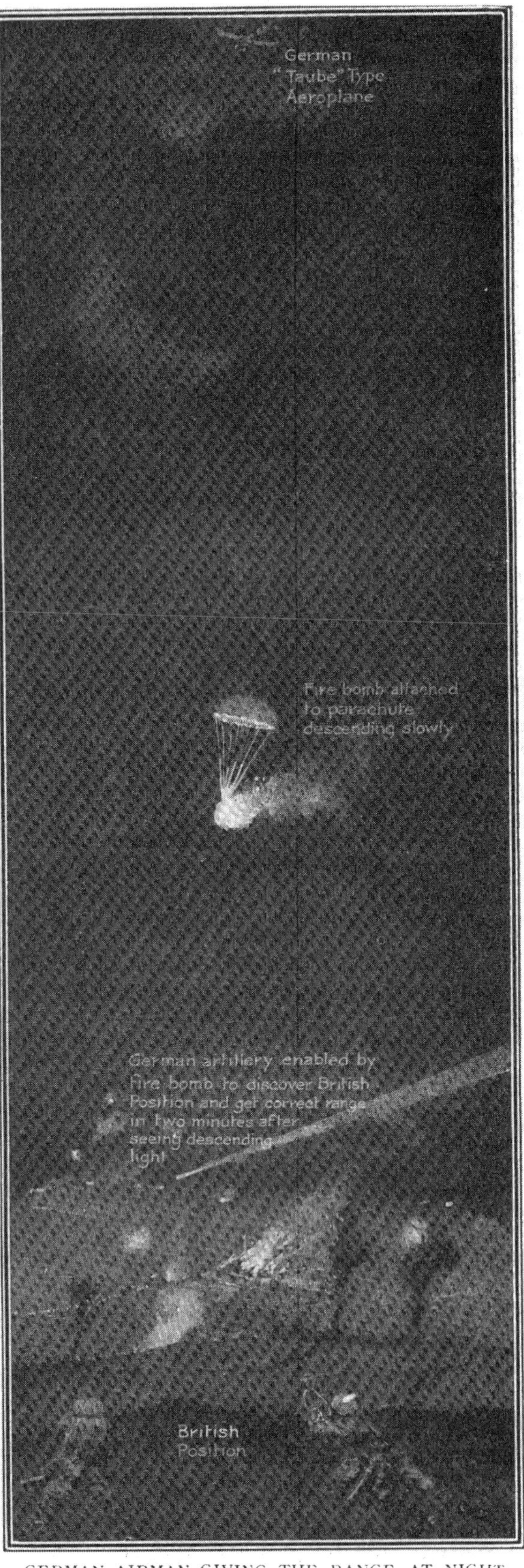

GERMAN AIRMAN GIVING THE RANGE AT NIGHT.

The Germans developed a system of fire-bombs dropped from aeroplanes to indicate to their gunners the positions to attack. The fire-bomb, attached to a parachute, shows a red light as it falls, and the German artillery attack the position immediately below.

THE ARTILLERY OF THE SKY.
The light aircraft are used for attack as well as for observation purposes. This picture illustrates how a shrapnel bomb bursts before reaching the ground and scatters over a comparatively wide area among the guns and men of the enemy.

though it had become twisted into a wavy line. This shows why such an elaborate outfit of apparatus and spare parts is required in the field with the flying wing of an army, including large motor workshops, huge motor-vans that carry numerous sets of spare wings stacked up like theatrical scenery, also portable sheds, and parts of all sorts.

War wastage of men and machines

Aircraft want much looking after. Even when used under peace conditions they have extremely short useful lives. Much more brief is their existence, therefore, under conditions of warfare, when it is scarcely possible to make a single flight for the purpose of observation without being subjected to fire of some sort. Hence the extraordinary rate at which Germany and France, and even our own factories, strove to produce machines to take the place of those at the front as fast as they were used up. The tragedy of the situation is that pilots are apt to get used up nearly as fast as their machines, and they can be made only by lengthy experience and tuition. A military pilot has to be very much more than a very good aerodrome performer and cross-country airman.

At the opening of war, Germany had about seven hundred qualified aeroplane pilots. Within two months of the outbreak of war she trained an extra hundred men in military flying near Berlin alone. Her activities were on a corresponding scale at her other flying centres. The German Government took over all the factories, flying-grounds, and airship sheds as soon as war was declared, so that it had at its disposal some three dozen centres at which to train pupils, apart from the big Army Flying Schools at Diedenhofen, Doeberitz, Metz, Oberwiesenfeld, Saarburg, and Sperenberg, and the Naval Flying Schools at Hollminsel and Putzig.

German training for airmen

Her military airmen were well exercised before the war in surprise calls. Without an instant's warning for men or machines, the Director of Military Aeronautics would issue orders for squadrons of three aeroplanes apiece to set out across country to a specified centre where they would all assemble, and then undertake other flights, as directed. It gave the Germans great faith in their air service that in all these rehearsals the journeys were made with extraordinary expedition and punctuality, and with no more waste of time in the starting than the fire brigade takes to turn out in London. There was no single accident or failure of any unit in such practice of the war game.

Germany also aimed very carefully at building up a big reserve of civilian pilots, whom she encouraged by promoting so-called touring and sporting competitions. These were divided into two sections—a military and a civilian one—with a military officer accompanying each civilian on his flight in the capacity of observer.

There were various tours of this description in East Prussia, precisely in the neighbourhood where Russia became so active, and along the French frontier. It is noteworthy that all these so-called pleasure cruises by air invariably involved flying over fortresses and reconnoitring a frontier. Sometimes the Emperor gave the chief prize for the military section, and the Crown Prince that for the civilian section. At other times Prince Henry of Prussia gave the chief awards.

German secrecy in air work

There was never any lack of handsome prizes, and all concerned were always made to realise very fully that the rulers of the country, from the Kaiser downwards, took the keenest personal interest in the achievement of every individual airman and constructer. In the absence of the international element, the world realised comparatively little of these activities. From start to finish it was the policy of the Government to focus the attention of the world on German prowess as represented by giant dirigibles. The Zeppelins incidentally served as an admirable

GERMAN AIRMEN FLYING OVER THE ALLIED ARMIES COULD INDICATE TO THEIR ARTILLERY THE—
The co-operation of airmen makes artillery fire much more effective than formerly. The airman flies out in front of the attacking line until he comes to the enemy's lines, above which he hovers, thereby indicating to his own side the locality of the opposing positions. A similar

mask for the rapid development of the aeroplane section, and also of lighter and smaller forms of airships—the Parseval frameless and collapsible dirigible balloons, of which Germany possess a good number, and the Gross, or semi-rigid type. Even so, it was believed by many that Germany contrived to build a considerable additional number of Zeppelin airships unknown to the outer world.

We must now consider her rate of construction of this single class of aircraft to be fully two dozen a year. Nor let it be imagined for a moment that they are as easily disposed of as newspaper reports would suggest. The first six weeks of warfare only resulted in the proved capture of two Zeppelins, and at her normal rate of manufacture just stated she had in these weeks made good this war wastage. As our history of the war develops we shall see that they will be employed for scouting at sea, and for assisting German warships to pass safely through the British blockading cordon, and it was undoubtedly our weakness that we had so few dirigible balloons, and none of high speed and long range like the Zeppelins.

Against them our battleships went to war armed with high-angle guns. But we must remember that a Zeppelin can easily carry heavy and therefore very destructive missiles, and that she can fly well above the range even of high-angle guns, so that the only thing that can get above her is the seaplane. In this branch Britain was happily more than Germany's match.

In the matter of aeroplanes the French equipment was a match for the German, alike in number and skill of pilots and capacity of production. France, with her small scouting and short-range dirigibles, was certainly also a match for Germany in all classes of semi-rigid and frameless airships. She had, however, none of the Zeppelin class; but this class, over land as over water, can be outflown in every sense by the bomb-dropping aeroplane.

Number and quality of British airmen

Our aerial equipment was on a par, not with our Navy, the largest in the world, but with our Army, which constituted the minor portion of the forces engaged in France. We had a large number of fine airmen, and over eight hundred British pilots had taken their aviator's certificate. Quite five hundred of them were trained for the two Services, a large proportion for naval work. The difficult

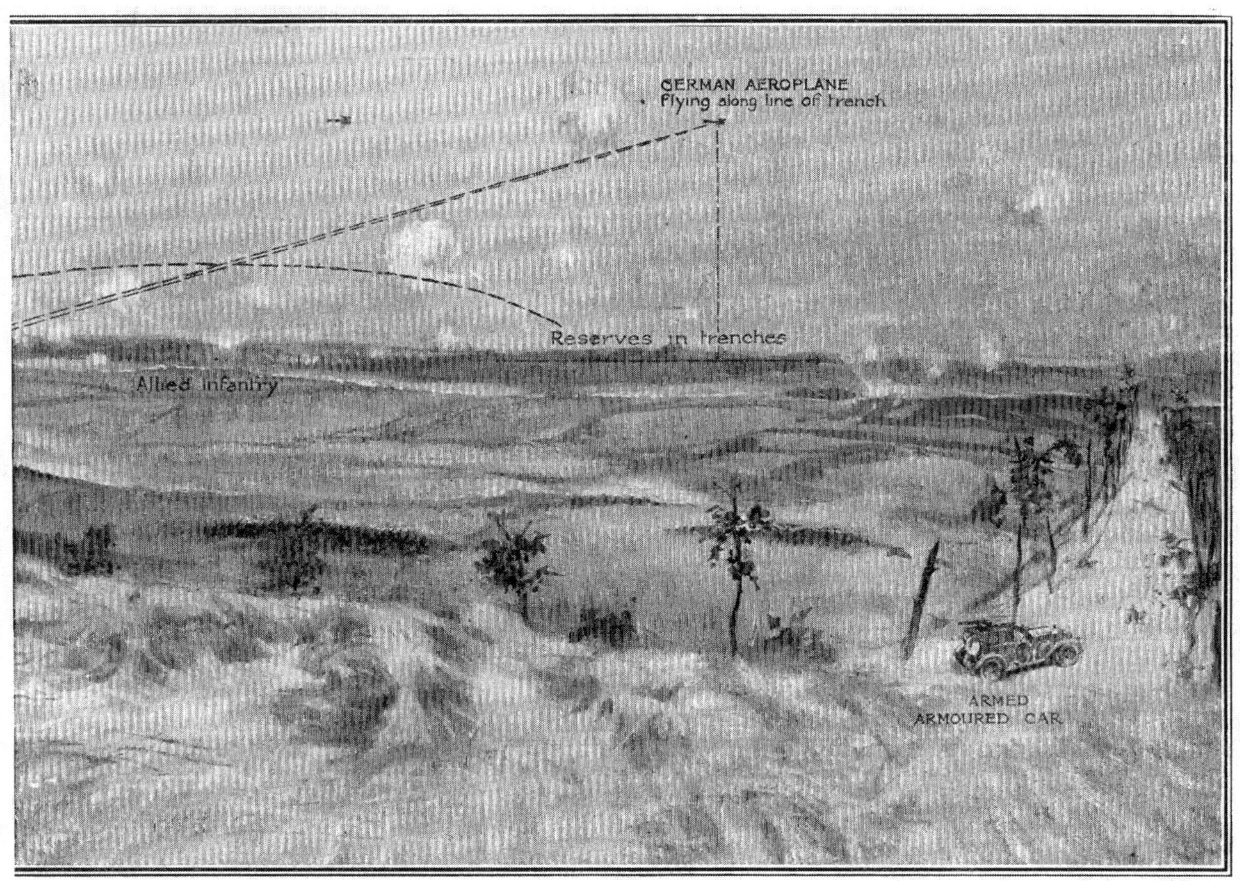

—ENEMY'S POSITIONS, THUS FINDING THE RANGE WHEN THE OBJECTS OF ATTACK REMAINED INVISIBLE.
service is also rendered during the hours of darkness by a system of lights, as explained on page 328. The picture above is sufficiently explanatory of the system of day observation. The inspecting officer reports to his colleagues, who telephone instructions to the concealed artillery.

nature of England as an aeroplaning country in these early stages of aerial development produced its own reward; flying over the Continent is easy by comparison.

Our airmen, like our seamen, could not be surpassed. It is not only that they have the right temperament and the physical skill, but also that their training is extremely thorough. Yet we must not lose sight of the fact that it takes a long time to train a civilian airman until he becomes an expert and serviceable military pilot. He has to scout at a height of 6,000 feet, or more than a mile, travelling at that altitude at probably an average of a mile a minute, accurately estimating the character and number of the enemy's dispositions and movements, as well as acting in co-operation with his own artillery, for which his advent has opened up new and undreamt-of possibilities. There is no blind groping for the range, or leaving it to chance. So long as there are airmen at the artillery's service, they can report by instant signal whether a shot has fallen short, far, or wide.

Little heed has been paid in this country to the Russian aerial equipment, yet so long ago as the Crimean War, Russia began to give attention to scouting by balloon. Since the coming of the aeroplane, Russian aviators

FIXING AN AIRSHIP'S PROPELLER 2,000 FEET ABOVE THE SEA.
A conspicuous act of bravery was performed in a British airship patrolling the Straits of Dover while our Expeditionary Force was crossing. The Secretary of the Admiralty's report ran as follows: "On one occasion it became necessary to change a propeller-blade. The captain feared he would have to descend for this purpose, but two of the crew immediately volunteered to carry out this difficult task in the air, and climbing out on to the bracket carrying the propeller shafting, they completed the hazardous work two thousand feet above the sea."

have proved extraordinarily skilful and daring. The Russian pilot Efimoff first found out how to "bank" (turn) abruptly with a Farman type of biplane. Russia, moreover, early placed important orders for dirigible balloons in France, Germany, and Italy; and she has a plant of her own for turning out aircraft.

At the outset, Germany had twice as many airships of various types as France, who came second in order with perhaps a score. Germany could show a greater number of trained military airmen and of military aeroplanes than any one country, having about one hundred in excess of France. By at once taking over all the motor and aircraft works in the Fatherland, and setting them to work at full capacity, she maintained her lead. Though various textbooks which have been published since the outbreak of war deal with her air equipment, perhaps we may be permitted to point out that the estimates of Germany's fleet of airships published are all much too low. Undoubtedly at the outbreak of war, Germany had at least forty-five rigid type of airships. But only a few of these were large Zeppelins. The majority were of about two-thirds the length of these monsters, but had a very high speed—not far short of a mile a minute—and a range of about 800 miles, as against 1,200.

Germany's ally, Austria, had no aircraft manufacturing capacity worthy of the name, though she made certain types of heavy, slow-speed aero-engines, and had one or two aeroplane works. So far as concerns her air fleet, Austria was not formidable. When her few dirigibles, including two or three of Zeppelin types, had been accounted for, she could scarcely rely on Germany, from whom she got such craft, to replace them. Certain of her semi-rigid types of airships of a really efficient character, such as she had purchased in France, could not be replaced from Germany during the war.

Comparative aircraft strength

The situation at the outset, therefore, was that Germany's aerial equipment was individually superior in numbers of all arms, including armoured motor-cars with high-angle guns, to any one country against which she was arrayed. But this was discounted by the fact that her energies had to be dissipated in campaigns against Russia, France, Belgium, and Britain on land and sea.

At the outbreak of war the Allies had as many airships as Germany and Austria, but they had none of the special Zeppelin type. They possessed in the Astra-Torres machines, such as France uses and such as our Navy employs, a highly efficient pattern which is particularly suitable for oversea work. The Allies had also, collectively, a greater number and variety of aeroplanes and a greater number of pilots, who between them combined a greater variety of experience. The Allies were therefore able to choose their pilots according to the work to be done, whereas the German airmen had to meet all Germany's rapidly changing needs.

The aerial situation, however, differs from the naval situation in one very essential point. Whereas it is impossible to create a navy during the war, if the foundations of an aerial force exist in the organisation and the

GERMAN EFFORTS TO BRING DOWN A BRITISH BIPLANE IN FRANCE.

A rough sketch of this scene was made by a British officer in France, and it was completed in London. The Germans were in a position behind the valley seen in front, and one after another the shells exploded as they attacked the Farman biplane manned by a member of the Royal Flying Corps, who went through the bombardment unhurt. Against the deep azure of the sky the shells exploded as white puffs, which became darker as they expanded. In rapid succession they came until more than half a dozen small clouds of smoke hung in mid-air, with the threatened aeroplane visible through their misty edges. The British troops in the foreground watched the German firing with intense interest.

SQUADRON-COMMANDER SPENSER GREY AFTER THE SECOND ATTACK ON THE DUSSELDORF AIRSHIP SHED.

Early in October, 1914, Squadron-Commander Spenser D. A Grey, R.N., accompanied by Lieutenants R. L. G. Marix and S V Sippe, made an attack upon the Düsseldorf airship shed. One bomb, dropped from a height of five hundred feet, hit the shed, went through the roof, and destroyed a Zeppelin. Flames were observed five hundred feet high, the result of igniting the escaping gas of the airship The feat was remarkable, having regard to the distance—over one hundred miles—penetrated into country held by the enemy, and to the fact that a previous attack had put the enemy on his guard and enabled him to mount anti-aircraft guns.

factories requisite, a very much larger aerial force can be created during the progress of a war. It is also possible to improve the aerial equipment, and replace it at a much greater rate than wastage can occur. The German plans recognised this. German productive capacity remains greater than that of any one country against which Germany was arrayed; but this is discounted by the fact that the Allies collectively had a far greater productive capacity under all headings.

Therefore, if by the wastage of war the Allies lost one machine and one man for each one lost by Germany, then, as the war lengthened, the more markedly could their aerial equipment preponderate, because they could create and replace more rapidly.

The scale on which building proceeded in Germany might be judged from the fact that, six weeks after the outbreak of war, it was officially announced at Berlin that three squadrons of airships were being laid down, and would be ready promptly. Doubtless this meant that the large number of airships laid down so successfully in secret would make a public appearance soon after. Further, Germany secured some 3,000 volunteers for her air service. The expansion of the German air fleet, however, was jeopardised by the awkward position of Germany and Austria in the matter of petrol supplies. The Russian successes in Galicia cut off one main source of supply, while the blockade prevented importation by sea. Moreover, up to April before the war, the petrol stocks of both countries were absolutely normal, so that no extraordinary reserves could have been accumulated against the outbreak of war. In any shortage of fuel

DAMAGED AEROPLANE NEAR NAMUR.

A French monoplane wrecked within the fighting area around Namur during the third week of August, 1914. The body of the machine was covered with thin steel, which had been dented by bullets. The engine has gone, and only the battered hood which encircled the revolving cylinders remains. The wheels have metal discs and the framework is steel throughout.

RUSSIAN AEROPLANE CAPTURED BY GERMANS AT LOTZEN.

As long ago as the Crimean War, Russia began to give attention to scouting by balloons, and since the coming of the aeroplane her aviators have shown particular initiative and daring. This photograph shows the remains of a Russian aeroplane, taken by the German General von Hindenburg at Lotzen, being removed on a transport waggon. The engine was afterwards fitted to and used in a German aeroplane.

BRITISH BIPLANE *VERSUS* GERMAN TAUBE.

The British Royal Flying Corps, from the beginning of its activity at the battle-front, made it their practice to challenge instantly any German airman appearing in the vicinity. Thus, air duels became of frequent occurrence, and British dash made most of them result in favour of the Allies. This special sketch portrays such an air duel, where a Bristol biplane, piloted by a member of the corps, manœuvred above a German Taube. A pistol fight followed, but attempts by German troops below to bring down the British aeroplane and a French Bleriot machine, that had joined in the sport, caused both the attackers to fly off.

the Third Arm would be the last to suffer. An army would sooner dispense with the use of motor-cars than lose its power of reconnoitring from the air.

Yet it did not follow that, because Germany possessed certain types of aircraft which the Allies lacked, the Allies were necessarily at a grave disadvantage. Germany aimed at supplying herself with the machines suited to her particular needs. But there was a vast difference between her requirements and those of any one of the Allies. Hence Great Britain's employment of moderate sized airships, even for naval work, and her adaption, for land warfare on a small scale, of readily portable airships, such as are the least extravagant to keep and the hardiest to withstand weather.

The weak point in the British aeroplane equipment at the outset lay in its dependence on foreign motors. But from the moment war was declared, the necessary measures were taken to remedy this defect, and to profit by the lessons of the Government Aero-Engine Competition, held in the summer of 1914. This was prematurely closed on the outbreak of war—which did not come, however, until the tests had been in progress for more than two months. A great deal of valuable knowledge had been gleaned, with the result that some of the largest British motor factories are working day and night supplying engines of suitable types. The Navy was particularly to be congratulated on the style of motors reaching it as the result of the orders given.

The question of aircraft motors

If Germany obtained a splendid rally of recruits to replace wastage in her air service, the Allies could show even better results. The military training schools in France were full of pupils, and our own aviation centres were working to their utmost capacity on sensible lines. Nor was there any dearth of further volunteers as time went on.

During the first two months of the war the Third Arm was used in an extraordinarily wide variety of ways, and thoroughly established itself. The first problem was the safe transport of the British Expeditionary Force. Convoying by warship is useful, but is limited by the fact that the warship travels on the same plane, and is practically subjected to the same restricted range of vision as the transports it is meant to shield.

HOW THE PARISIANS REGARDED THE MOVEMENTS OF A GERMAN AEROPLANE.
Interest in the spectacle overrides any feeling of personal danger when a hostile aeroplane appears over a city. Every man or woman realises that his or her chance of injury from the falling bomb is small. This photograph was taken in Paris when a German "Taube" was hovering above.

"5 minutes make the difference between victory and defeat!"

—LORD NELSON

THIS is an age of petrol. Swift action, swift transport, will be a deciding factor in the present titanic upheaval in Europe.

In an important engagement it is easily conceivable that immortal Nelson's dictum will be signally exemplified in the present struggle. Motor-haulage of field-guns has proved very successful in manœuvres. How successful it will be in actual warfare we are yet to see.

In all questions of motor traction the fuel plays a vital part.

PRATT'S

Motor Spirit

is used by War Office and Admiralty for motor-cars, aeroplanes, seaplanes, and on the waters for petrol-driven craft. The choice of Pratt's Spirit for this important work is a significant tribute to its sheer merit and consistent reliability. Pratt's also enjoys the complete confidence of our Allies, who are using it in enormous quantities.

In Peace as in War, Pratt's Spirit is the motorist's first and final choice because of its unrivalled power and purity.

ANGLO-AMERICAN OIL COMPANY, LTD.,
36, Queen Anne's Gate, London, S.W.

By Appointment.

A Printed and published by the AMALGAMATED PRESS, LIMITED, The Fleetway House, Farringdon Street, London, E.C.
Published by Gordon & Gotch in Australia and New Zealand; by The Central News Agency, Ltd., in South Africa; by The Standard Literature Co., 13/1, Old Court House Street, Calcutta; and The Imperial News Co., Toronto and Montreal in Canada. *Advertisement applications should be made to The Advertisement Manager, The Fleetway House, Farringdon Street, London, E.C*

With the Publishers' Cases Only

Artistic title-page and index to volume, splendid frontispiece consisting of a fine photogravure of Admiral Jellicoe

Not only are the publishers' cases the best value obtainable, but readers who secure them will have the satisfaction of knowing that with them ***and with them only*** will be given an artistic title-page and index to the volume, and a splendid frontispiece for the volume, consisting of a magnificent photogravure portrait of Admiral Jellicoe.

THE GREAT WAR as a book, therefore, is not complete without the publishers' registered cases, for in no other way can one obtain these additions so necessary to the completeness of a beautiful book.

For those whose choice must be Cloth or nothing, the publishers are issuing, at the very low price of 2/6, the exceedingly serviceable case illustrated below, which is as good as cloth binding can be.

This case is made of the best English cloth, described by binders as "full cloth extra." It is of a rich wine colour, and bears a handsome design blocked in black on the side, while the title on the back is in gold. The boards are extra thick, with bevelled edges.

As has already been stated, Half Leather binding is the best value and should be secured by all who can possibly afford it, but it is better to get even the Cloth than to let the parts lie about and become tattered and torn.

Whichever binding you choose, do it now!

ABOUT THE AUTHOR

Mark Bussler is a writer, artist, and filmmaker specializing in video game, history, and science fiction related projects across a broad spectrum of media. Mark created ***Classic Game Room*** in 1999, and it remains the longest-running Internet video game review show in the world.

He writes retro game collecting and review guides based on the Classic Game Room museum archives. Mark is also the creator, writer and artist of several comic book series including *Ethel the Cyborg Ninja, Heyzoos the Coked-Up Chicken, Lord Karnage, Magnum Skywolf, Surf Panda, Retromegatrex* and *Turbo Volcano*. He draws digitally using a combination of iPad Pro and Wacom tools in Adobe Photoshop.

Mark scanned the complete *The Great War: The Standard History of the All-Europe Conflict* and remastered them for future generations in this collection.

Follow Mark Bussler on Amazon for new book updates!

www.Amazon.com/author/MarkBussler

Subscribe to all my channels!

www.ClassicGameRoom.com
www.Amazon.com/v/ClassicGameRoom
www.Patreon.com/ClassicGameRoom
www.Instagram.com/ClassicGameRoom
www.Twitter.com/ClassicGameRoom

Mark's T-Shirts can be found on Amazon.com by searching
TURBO VOLCANO

Continued in
THE GREAT WAR:
Remastered WW1 Standard History Collection
Volume 5

OTHER BOOKS & GRAPHIC NOVELS BY MARK BUSSLER

Ultra Massive Video Game Console Guide Volume 1

Ultra Massive Video Game Console Guide Volume 2

Ethel the Cyborg Ninja Book 1

The Great War: Remastered WWI Standard History Collection

Lord Karnage 1.5 Special Edition

Retromegatrex Volume 1: The Lost Art of Mark Bussler 1995-2017

Heyzoos the Coked-Up Chicken #1 Special Edition

Heyzoos the Coked-Up Chicken #2 Special Edition

Surf Panda #1

How To Make A Video Game Review Show That Doesn't Suck

World's Fair of 1893 Ultra Massive Photographic Adventure

The White City of Color: 1893 World's Fair

Pac-Man Collector's Guide: A Definitive Review

Classic Game Room's Nintendo Switch Collector's Review Guide

Old Timey Pictures With Silly Captions Volume 1

Old Timey Pictures With Silly Captions Volume 2

www.ClassicGameRoom.com

Printed in Great Britain
by Amazon

30203450R00057